P9-CKT-761

Twayne's English Authors Series

Sylvia E. Bowman, *Editor*

INDIANA UNIVERSITY

*Peter Pindar
(John Wolcot)*

(TEAS) 155

PETER PINDAR
(JOHN WOLCOT)

By Robert L. Vales

Gannon College

Twayne Publishers, Inc. :: New York

Preface

"Peter Pindar" (John Wolcot) is a topical satirist who is unfamiliar to many readers though his numerous works were best sellers in the eighteenth century. His success was due, in part, to his attacks on such prominent figures as William Pitt, Thomas Paine, and George III, to mention but a few. He was regarded as frank, vulgar, and too personal by some critics, but he is the most important satirist between Jonathan Swift and Lord Byron. His political satires perhaps aid in accounting for the decline of satire since the shift from general folly to particular personalities limits the scope of attack, and the personal rather than the universal is stressed. This emphasis on topicality also accounts for Wolcot's current obscurity. He, however, has moments of such humor and irony that he is worthy of being read for the sheer enjoyment of his wit, but not all of his works contain such moments.

Wolcot was a prolific writer. Counting each of the five cantos of *The Lousiad* as an individual work, since each appeared separately between 1785 and 1795, the *Cambridge Bibliography of English Literature* lists sixty-one satires by John Wolcot, five miscellanies of serious and humorous poems, two serious poetical works, two books which he edited, one play, and probably three pieces of questioned authorship (see Selected Bibliography). The satires issued in quarto pamphlets vary in length, and their contents and structure vary also. A work such as *Bozzy and Piozzi* (1786) deals entirely with Samuel Johnson's biographers and contains no additional poems, tales, or fables; but *More Money!* (1792) has a number of miscellaneous pieces and no controlling device to link them together. John Wolcot frequently expanded a satire through the addition of material which did not always pertain to his subject at hand.

Because Wolcott was a topical satirist, his times or his motivations for writing must be examined if his work is to be fully understood; therefore, a historical and biographical approach must necessarily be used as well as quotations and synopses since his works are not household bibles. Wolcot was primarily interested in public personalities, but many of the minor figures mentioned are hardly known today, and material to identify them has been taken from the *Dictionary of National Biography* which will not be footnoted unless information is quoted from this source. The satires dealing with publicly prominent individuals can be grouped together and examined as a unit if such a grouping is based on their occupation such as painter or writer. Within each chapter, the chronological order of the satires is maintained; and the dates affixed to a satire refer to the month of the earliest review, most frequently that of the *Monthly Review*.

Satire, in its simplest sense, is a criticism of someone or something. The satirist is then a critic examining and revealing faults; but it must be understood that these faults, follies, and vices are often seen only by the satirist. If one accepts the idea that a satirist is a critic, the question of author and personation can be disregarded by merely examining the person or the thing criticized and the manner and the form which the criticism takes. Peter Pindar as critic, a reporter on public personalities since he wrote topical satire, and his methods of criticism are the motif which guides each chapter and which unite all the satires under examination.

The structure of this study, therefore, will be a discussion of the topical satires listed under headings based primarily on the profession of the individuals under attack. The satirist as critic gives each chapter its form and necessitates statements concerning point of view and method of presentation. The first chapter reveals facts of John Wolcot's life, and the last one summarizes his talents and literary contribution.

Due to space limitations and the unfamiliarity of many readers with Peter Pindar's satires, this book is offered as an introduction to Wolcot's works for the general reader, the student, and the teacher. For additional biographical information, the selected bibliography should be consulted; lack of biographical works has made the bibliography brief, but other sources of information can be found in the notes to each chapter.

Because Wolcot revised his quarto pamphlets for their octavo publications, the 1812 edition of his works has been used. The 1816 edition, a sixteenmo, has smaller type and contains (except for one minor and forgettable poem, *Anticipation: An Address to be Spoken at the Opening of Drury Lane Theatre by a Landlord in the Character of Peter Puncheon*) the same works of the more easily read 1812 edition. The 1812 edition more closely approximates the quarto pamphlets. Poems found only in manuscript have been omitted from this study, and Wolcot's serious poems are only briefly mentioned and deserve to be so treated.

I am indebted to Professors W. Powell Jones and Harlan W. Hamilton whose guidance and criticism have proved invaluable. The resources and the librarians of the following libraries were most helpful: British Museum, Cleveland Public Library, Falmouth Library, Freiberger Library of Case-Western Reserve University, and the Library of Congress. This study received its initial impetus at Western Reserve University.

Contents

Chronology

1738   John Wolcot born in Dodbrooke; baptized May 9, Kingsbridge, Devonshire.

1751   Death of father; removal to uncle's home in Fowey, Cornwall.

1755   Graduates from Leskerard Grammar School; apprenticed to his uncle, a surgeon-apothecary.

1761   Year's residence in France.

1762–   Studies medicine in London.
1764

1767   September 8, receives medical degree from the University of Aberdeen.

1768   Sails to Jamaica as Sir William Trelawney's family physician.

1769   June 24, in London; becomes deacon in the Anglican church and a priest the following day.

1773   *Persian Love Elegies, to which is Added the Nymph of Tauris* (Kingston, Jamaica); returns to England.

1773   Practices medicine in Truro, Cornwall. Publishes satires on Truro
1779   citizens. Discovers and trains painter John Opie.

1781   Arrives with Opie in London; establishes him as a painter.

1782   *Lyric Odes to the Royal Academicians.* First use of the pseudonym "Peter Pindar."

1788   One-volume edition of Peter Pindar's works appears in Dublin— probably a pirated edition.

1792   In Dublin, two-volume pirated edition of his works appears.

1793   Winter of 1793–94, booksellers Robinson, Goulding, and Walker purchase Wolcot's copyright.

1794   *Works of Peter Pindar* in three volumes.

1800   Quarrel with William Gifford.

1807   June 27, tried and acquitted of charge of adultery.

1811   Loss of sight in right eye following operation.

1812   *Works of Peter Pindar* in five volumes.

1816   *Works of Peter Pindar* in four volumes.

1817   *A Most Solemn Epistle to the Emperor of China,* his last satire and the first to carry his true name.

1819   Dies January 14; buried in St. Paul's Church, Covent Garden.

CHAPTER 1

John Wolcot's Life

T HE exact date of John Wolcot's birth in Dodbrooke, Devonshire,
is unavailable; but the parish register in the neighboring town of
Kingsbridge reveals that he was baptized on May 9, 1738. The fourth
child of Alexander Wolcot, a surgeon, John attended the Kingsbridge Grammar School until his father's death in 1751. The family
moved to Fowey in Cornwall where the boy was placed in the care of
his uncle John, a surgeon-apothecary in that small community. The
boy must have found life unpleasant in his uncle's home because of
the presence of the uncle's sisters, who kept the house for their
brother. Later in life, Wolcot remarked to his friend John Taylor
"that he was kept under rigid control by two aunts, who cowed his
spirit to such a degree, that though he had been long released from
their tyranny, he never should think himself a man."[1]

I Medicine, Travel, Poetry

At the age of seventeen, after graduating from the Leskerard
Grammar School where he acquired a knowledge of Latin and
Greek, a proclivity for versifying, and an amateur skill in art, John
Wolcot was apprenticed to his uncle though he disliked apothecary
duties and preferred writing verses to such local girls as Miss
Coryton and Betsy Cranch. His early years, and later years, spent in
rural communities, account for his denigratory animal similes and
metaphors in his satires; barnyard fowls and pigs were used for
invidious comparisons. In 1761, at the completion of his apprenticeship, the uncle sent his twenty-three-year-old nephew to France to
learn the language. Information concerning his year's residence
there is unavailable, but his poems reveal that he acquired an
antipathy toward France and its people (see Chapter 6). On his return
to England, he followed his uncle's wishes and studied medicine in
London for two years. Returning to Fowey in 1764 without a medical
degree, he assisted his uncle and again wrote verses to the ladies;
but his poetry did not win him Susan Nankivell, who rejected his
offer of marriage. Pressure from his uncle finally led Wolcot to seek

the medical degree which was granted to him from the University of
Aberdeen on September 8, 1767.[2]

Among his uncle's patients at Fowey were members of the Trelawney family; and, when Sir William Trelawney was appointed
governor of Jamaica, John applied for and received the position of
physician to the governor's family. A letter to Benjamin Nankivell,
dated December 3, 1767, explains his desire to escape from the role
of poor relative and to have his own private funds—a desire which
later accounted for his writing satires which sold. He writes, "Ah!
Benjy it is not the idea of grandeur but of independence that seduces
me from Great Britain, or I should rather say from old England; the
hope of placing myself, by the labour of a few years beyond the
caprice of a mob." As part of Governor Trelawney's entourage, Wolcot was introduced at court; and the same letter states that, when
he went there on St. Andrew's Day, his sword caught between his
legs, sending him stumbling, much to the crowd's amusement. To
build up his courage and to calm his mind, he mentally engaged
"on a philosophical analysis of nobility or title" which he found to
mean nothing and "sat it down with myself as a general axiom, the
greater the man, the greater the fool. Fraught with these emotions
I went forth to see the King and the Queen and the Prince and
the Princesses, and the Duke and the Duchesses, etc. etc. etc.—
and behold I saw them!—and behold I never desire to see them
more!!—" This attitude of not being impressed by important
persons, stemming from embarrassment over a trivial incident, may
account for Wolcot's future satirical views of King George III (see
Chapters 8 and 9).

On August 7, 1768, Governor Trelawney's entourage left England,
stopped at various island ports, and arrived in October at Port Royal.
In Jamaica, an event occurred which later affected Wolcot's life. On
April 21, 1769, William Glanville Boscawen, a young naval
lieutenant, drowned while swimming in a pond. Wolcot wrote an
elegy on the youth's death and submitted it to the *Annual Register,*
a London periodical, where it gathered dust in that magazine's office
for ten years until the boy's mother discovered it and had it printed.

In Jamaica, John's income was small, and his duties light; but, as
a wit and as an official greeter of visiting dignitaries for the governor,
John a rather handsome, sensual-appearing man became a favorite
of Sir William. When the parish of St. Anne, worth twelve hundred
pounds to fifteen hundred pounds a year to its holder, was soon to

be vacant, Sir William suggested that John become a priest in order to receive that living. Wolcot appears to have had no professed religion, but he did wish to be an independent man; therefore, he sailed for England where on June 24, 1769, Richard Terry, bishop of London, ordained him a deacon of the church and, on the following day, a priest. Delayed in England settling legal formalities connected with his uncle's death in October, 1769, Wolcot did not return to Jamaica until March, 1770, only to discover that the incumbent of St. Anne's had recovered. This recovery meant that the new clergyman had to settle for the minor living of eight hundred pounds at Vere, a community of six thousand Negroes employed in that area's sugar mills and one in which the parishioners went to market on Sunday and not to church services. Frequently, when this newly ordained priest found his church empty on the Sabbath, he went hunting. Life at Vere for the well-educated, rather worldly and gregarious Wolcot was boring; and he soon appointed a deputy; returned to St. Jago de la Vega, the seat of the government; and resumed his duties connected with Sir William. This move ended Wolcot's clerical career. The only influence, a tenuous one, that such an experience had upon him appears in his later satires which occasionally use biblical metaphors and attack hypocrisy.

Shortly after Wolcot rejoined Sir William, the governor's sister Anne died, and Wolcot wrote an elegy on her death entitled *The Nymph of Tauris,* which the 1773 *Annual Register* (240–41) published. He had written other verses, and they appeared to have had some value in that island community, for Joseph Thompson of Kingston, Jamaica, published Wolcot's *Persian Love Elegies* (1773) which included the poem to the memory of Anne Trelawney. Though the poems suggest the influence of William Collins, they are so similar to other eighteenth-century verse in style and in sentiment that they do not merit serious consideration. It is sufficient to note that Wolcot was writing poetry and that his earliest interest was in serious verse, not in the satire for which he later became famous.

II *The Return to England*

When Sir William died on December 11, 1772, Wolcot was given permission to accompany Lady Letitia Trelawney, the widow, back to England; and Wolcot never returned to Jamaica. About the only tangible items Wolcot recieved from his Jamaican adventures were permanent skin discoloration, asthma, an occasional reference to the alligator in his satires, and wonderment at man's credulousness. He would test a person's credulity with a tale that in Jamaica a cherubim and a seraphim had been captured and placed in the same cage; unfortunately, they had fought, had destroyed each other, and had had to be buried. John Taylor, attempting to assess the satirist's character, wrote that "Dr. Wolcot had been in various parts of the world, and had mixed with all the different classes of mankind, the result of which intercourse was, a very unfavourable opinion of human nature."[4]

From 1773 to 1779, Wolcot established his medical practice at Truro, Cornwall, and its environs where his methods, unusual according to the standards of the time, aroused the ire of his fellow practitioners. He advocated cold water for fevers; felt that a doctor should aid nature sparingly; and, more important, examined the prescriptions he ordered to insure that the apothecaries had not substituted cheaper ingredients. In these actions, we see two attitudes of the future satirist: a belief in common sense and nature plus a distrust of his fellow man. But Wolcot was a pleasant, genial man with friends. Richard Polwhele, who attended the school at Truro at this time, said "the wit and pleasantry of Wolcot's conversation would always render him a welcome visitor at the houses of all his acquaintances in Truro and the neighborhood."[5] The Truro Town Council and Henry Rosewarne, Member of Parliament for the borough, among others, held a different opinion since they became the subject for much of Wolcot's satirical wit. This wit and his medical practices earned him only animosity, and an attempt was made to inform him that those in authority had many means to retaliate. Lacking an apprentice, Wolcot was sent a letter by John Buckland, overseer of Truro, on November 28, 1779, requesting him to appear the next day for a drawing of apprentices or to show cause why he should not have an apprentice.[6] Wolcot, instead, gave up his medical practice and moved to nearby Helstone; for he had formed ambitious plans connected with John Opie (1761–1807), the young portrait and historical painter whom he had discovered.

Once while on his medical rounds, Wolcot visited the Nankivelles, the parents of his former sweetheart; and he saw there some crude drawings by a fifteen-year-old boy named John Opie, a minecarpenter's apprentice. Expressing an interest in the drawings,

Wolcot soon met Opie, saw that the boy had talent, gave him painting materials, and took him in charge. It must be mentioned that Wolcot had some talent as an artist, for several of his land-scapes were printed in 1797; he had also some critical ability, for he wrote the article on Richard Wilson for Matthew Pilkington's *Dictionary of Painters* (1799). According to Ada Earland, an Opie biographer, "Wolcot's art-teaching was, like himself, shrewd and sensible. His lessons were chiefly in crayons. He made no effort to confine Opie's genius within conventional channels. Originality was not stifled: he was more concerned with guiding a natural force than in attempting impossibilities by insisting on the artificial grace then considered an essential in portraiture."[7] Opie received lessons not only in art from the doctor but also in manners, though the boy never progressed very far in the latter. Wolcot sent the youth off as an itinerant portrait painter, and Opie's talents soon bloomed to such an extent that both master and pupil felt ready to attack London. An informal agreement was made whereby the earnings Wolcot received from his pen and those Opie received from his brush were to be shared equally. With this agreement, Wolcot's medical career ended; and he again sought independence and freedom from the caprice of the mob.

In the autumn of 1781, they arrived in London, and Wolcot became Opie's press agent. He touted the boy as an untaught genius and made him wear a green feather in his hat to set him apart. Luck now aided Wolcot, for his *Elegy* on young Boscawen had been discovered by the boy's mother and was printed in the *Annual Register* for 1779. Learning that Wolcot was in town, Mrs. Boscawen invited him to visit her, and Wolcot introduced her to his young painter with much praise of the boy's talents. Mrs. Boscawen recommended Opie to her friends, and he was soon a success: "Wolcot had not overestimated the attraction of an oddity. Opie's lodgings in Orange Court were soon besieged by a fashionable crowd eager to have the reputation of sitting to the new artist." Opie married and was highly successful (he became a member of the Royal Academy in 1787), but Wolcot was not yet a success as a writer when Opie's newly acquired relatives persuaded the painter to divest himself from all ties and bargains made with his mentor. Wolcot and Opie separated but remained on good terms; later, however, Opie only charged the doctor for the canvas when he painted his portrait.

III *The Emergence of Peter Pindar*

Now, to all appearances, Wolcot disappeared; and Peter Pindar, Esquire, emerged. The London he had entered was filled with the productions of caricaturists and satirists, and Wolcot was no stranger to satire. Earlier he had published anonymously two satires, *The Noble Criketeers* (1778) and *An Epistle to the Reviewers* (1778), which had attracted little attention. Now his circumstances in London, his knowledge of painting, his connection with Opie, and the annual exhibition of the paintings of the Royal Academy led to *Lyric Odes to the Royal Academicians* (1782) "by Peter Pindar, Esq., a distant Relation to the Poet of Thebes, and Laureat to the Academy." Wolcot exercised his critical abilities in praising Sir Joshua Reynolds and in attacking such artists as Benjamin West and Angelica Kauffmann, but the satire was not eagerly purchased by the public. *More Lyric Odes to the Royal Academicians* (1783) had a larger sale, and the quarto-size satirical pamphlets of Peter Pindar soon became best sellers. He did not write true Pindaric odes, and the fact that both poets left the country to earn fame in the city makes only a lame comparison. Perhaps Wolcot's own statement in the 1782 *Odes* comes closest to the truth, for it reveals the miscellaneous nature of his verse:

> My Cousin Pindar, in his Odes,
> Applauded Horse-jockeys and Gods,
> Wrestlers and Boxers, in his Verse divine:
> Then shall not I, who boast his fire,
> An old hereditary Lyre,
> To British Painters give a golden Line?   (Ode I, 1-6)

There appears to be no discernible influence by the Theban poet upon Peter Pindar's writing; but an influence upon the poet's style and methods can be found in *The Beauties of English Poetry* (1804), which was edited by Wolcot. Most of the humorous pieces in this two-volume collection of minor verse are by Wolcot and had appeared previously in his satires; but it is *An Heroic Epistle to Sir William Chambers* by William Mason (1724–97), printed in this collection without an author's name, which shows a decided influence upon the satirist. William Chambers's *A Dissertation on Oriental Gardening* (1772), which praised Eastern gardening above English landscape gardening, prompted Mason's satire which appeared in 1772 under the pseudonym of Malcolm Macgregor.[9]

While mocking Chamber's taste, Mason imaginatively presents the effect of Chamber's thesis if it were completely followed. Pagodas would rise in gardens in which animals from the monkey to the elephant would range; and, to add to the terrors, gibbets would also be erected. Mason's conclusion, requesting the post of official bard to this architect, sounds quite similar to many of Peter Pindar's lines. Mason writes:

> And thou, Sir William! while thy plastic hand
> Creates each wonder, which thy bard has plann'd;
> While, as thy art commands, obsequious rise
> Whate'er can please, or frighten, or surprise,
> O! let the bard his Knight's protection claim,
> And share, like faithful, Quixote's fame.
>
> (ll. 141–46)

Certain parallels to Wolcot's methods are evident in Mason's satire: the basing of a poem on an immediate event or literary work, the mock praise, the good-natured tone, the imaginative creation of such a work's effect, and the conclusion which damns the intellect of the human subject. Whether Wolcot consciously or unconsciously imitated Mason's methods cannot be ascertained, but it seems significant that he chose this work for inclusion in *The Beauties of English Poetry*. In any case, John Wolcot's criticism, wit, irony, similes, and manner found favor after 1783 with the public; success followed success. A. S. Collins says that "the only man who really made money by poetry in the last decades of the eighteenth century was Wolcot." The price of his satires rose from one shilling to half a crown in 1785, and pirated editions began to appear in Dublin in 1788 and 1792. Piracy of his work reached such a height that his publishers began offering a ten- and later a twenty-guinea reward for information leading to the arrest and conviction of persons engaged in such theft.

Wolcott, though he attacked folly and stressed neoclassic ideals in his criticism, wished first of all to make money; any topical event or public personality was suitable for his purpose. He attacked Samuel Johnson's biographers, George III, William Pitt, Sir Joseph Banks (the president of the Royal Society), and many others. During the period when he was the reigning satirist of London, Wolcot, a frequenter of many clubs, was the friend of painters, sculptors, actors, and musicians from whom he received information about the great which he used in his satires. Depending on the nature of his audience, he was viewed as either coarse or genial; but he was also known to be nervous in the presence of a title—and his old feeling of inferiority was overcome only by adopting a blustering manner. His success produced imitators, attacks, and even fears on his part that the government would bring libel action against him. In *Peter's Pension* (1788), Wolcot claimed the government had offered him a pension if he would cease attacking the monarch, but he had refused the bribe. This claim appears to be a fabrication, and it may have been intended to offer the government a clue that the poet might consider an annuity of some kind. When he did seek a pension in 1795, he promised to write pro-administration pieces; but he disavowed the entire transaction in a dispute over the amount to be received. Still the search for independence guided him. On November 14, 1791, he had written to Thomas Giddy, "Thank God there is an asiatic famine in poetry. Now is your time to write verses. I daily compose some nonsense, and am lucky to meet with fools to buy it."[11]

From June, 1973, to February, 1796, he occasionally wrote literary criticism for the *Monthly Review*. Contrary to the image Wolcot created as Peter Pindar, as a caustic but genial critic, he acted in these book reviews the gentleman toward female writers; and, as for the males, he merely wished they would cease writing as if for oblivion. His own works sold so well that Robinson, Goulding, and Walker, a group of London booksellers, approached him during the winter of 1793–94 with an offer to purchase his copyright. Wolcot accepted an annuity of two hundred and fifty pounds which he received until his death.

Wolcot had acquired a bit of an international reputation by now. General Tadeusz Kosciuszko, who was a volunteer in the American Continental Army and who later fought for the liberation of Poland, read Wolcot's works. After being imprisoned from December, 1794, to November, 1796, in St. Petersburg by the Russians for leading Polish insurgents, Kosciuszko traveled through Sweden and Finland to England; and, upon reaching London on May 30, 1797, he asked Peter Pindar to call on him. Kosciuszko told Wolcot that the satires of Peter Pindar had helped sustain him in prison and that he was pleased with the freedom in England which allowed the great to be attacked.

When Wolcot satirized Hannah More in *Nil Admirari* (1799), the

Anti-Jacobin Magazine and Review attacked him as a monster interested only in vice and scandal. "John Gifford" (John Richards Green), editor of the periodical, was responsible for its contents; but Wolcot mistakenly assumed that William Gifford (1756–1826), the author of the *Baviad* and the *Maeviad* who had been connected with that periodical when it was first issued, was responsible for the review. Wolcot disparaged Gifford's character in a postscript to *Lord Auckland's Triumph* (1800), and William Gifford replied in July, 1800, with *An Epistle to Peter Pindar*. In Gifford's prose introduction to the *Epistle* he called Peter's verse doggerel; and he declared that he did not fear "so feeble, so odious, so contemptible, so utterly despicable an object as Peter Pindar" (17). In the heroic couplets which followed, he described Wolcot as "A bloated mass, a gross un-kneaded clod,/ A foe to man, a renegade from God" (ll. 67–68), who as a child had destroyed insects and birds. Referring to the Jamaican days, Gifford claimed that even the Negroes were disgusted with "the prodigy of drunkenness and lust" (1.98). After Peter was expelled from Cornwall, he had gone to London where he "spung'd on dirty whores for dirty bread" (1.124). After warning Wolcot to mend his ways before his death, Gifford concluded that mere words could not express his scorn and hatred of the man.

Wolcot wrote a threatening letter to Gifford who replied that he would reveal more facts of a despicable nature relating to Peter Pindar. This exchange led to the encounter which one anonymous satirist wrote of as "The Battle of the Bards." Various accounts of the affair exist, but there is agreement on the following matters. On August 18, 1800, Wolcot entered Wright's bookshop, asked if William Gifford were the man before him, received an affirmative, and then struck him on the head with his cane. Gifford wrestled the stick from Wolcot's hand, drubbed him at least twice, and pushed Wolcot out of the bookshop door, making him lose his hat, cane, wig, and some blood. Wolcot later learned that Gifford was not the editor of the *Anti-Jacobin Magazine and Review,* but he never apologized for his actions.

After 1800, although Wolcot was beginning to lose touch with what the public wanted; and, although he suffered ill health and failing eyesight due to cataracts in both eyes, he was still writing and still being read. The most startling event during this period of his life occurred when, at the age of sixty-nine, he was charged with criminal conversation (adultery). Since his arrival in London, he had always lived in rented rooms, and on June 27, 1807, his current landlord charged that his wife had been seduced by the satirist. A full account of the court trial is given in the anonymous pamphlet *The Trial of Peter Pindar for Criminal Conversation* (1807), but the "Chronicle" section (449–53) of the *Annual Register* for 1807 presents the most succinct and accessible report. Mr. Knight, the landlord, brought the charges; the principal witnesses for the prosecution were Elizabeth Carter, servant, and Mrs. Pyke, lodger. The evidence, based on what these women claimed to have seen and heard, was circumstantial; its central point was that Wolcot had seduced the twenty-six-year-old Mrs. Knight while pretending to teach her how to become an actress. Mr. Parke, Wolcot's attorney, called the entire affair a conspiracy: "the defendant was upwards of seventy, blind, asthmatic, and a very antidote to love" (453). What was more pertinent to the case, the lawyer added, was that the defendant was physically incapable of the crime. After a brief conference, the jury found Wolcot innocent. Needless to say, Wolcot had moved to different lodgings.

By May, 1811, the satirist was nearly blind.[12] In an attempt to improve Wolcot's condition, Sir William Adams operated on his right eye in 1814; but Wolcot completely lost the sight in that eye soon after the operation.[13] Despite his near blindness in the left eye, Wolcot continued to compose satires, writing them himself or dictating to someone; but only one satire was published after this date. His works, however, were still being read, at least in the 1812 or 1816 collected editions. Mary Shelley recorded in her journal for Saturday, September 28, 1816, that Shelley had read aloud from the satirist's book.[14] Wolcot who was still somewhat socially active, was dining with some interesting individuals; for Mary Shelley records that on Wednesday, May 28, 1817, William Godwin and William Hazlitt had dined with the satirist.[15]

The verses which Wolcot wrote during this period were never published; they were sold after his death on January 14, 1819, but his papers and manuscripts have disappeared (except for some manuscript material which was purchased by J. D. Enys and which can be found in the Falmouth public library in Cornwall, England). According to his wishes, Wolcot was buried in St. Paul's Church, Covent Garden, next to the remains of Samuel Butler. John Taylor, who appears to have seen him last, recorded Wolcot's final words.

When Taylor asked him if there were anything which he desired, the satirist replied, "Bring back my youth."[16]

What emerges from Wolcot's biography is a picture of a learned, witty, and perhaps lazy man eager to obtain money to gain independence. The London he entered in 1781 was filled with the productions of caricaturists and satirists, and the proceedings of public trials were printed in pamphlet form and hawked in the streets. Since satire sold well, as did pamphlets on topical events, Wolcot wrote satires of a topical nature and was eventually unable to escape from the role of satirist. What set him apart from his contemporary satirists was his good humor as well as his talent. Few of his subjects were offended; rather, they were amused by the man's skill and imagination. He could not stand pretension, hypocrisy, or lack of common sense, especially in the great; and his attacks gave the public what it seemingly wanted. He wrote topical satires, and his topicality accounts for his decline in reputation; but his topicality also indicates that a historical-biographical approach is the best means for understanding his satires.

CHAPTER 2

The Royal Academicians

JOHN Wolcot began his career in 1782 as Peter Pindar with a satire on the annual art exhibition of the recently formed Royal Academy of Arts, and he devoted himself to the exhibitors until 1785 when he turned his attention to other public figures. Wolcot's interest in painting through his own art training and his press-agent activities on Opie's behalf perhaps accounts for the first satire by Peter Pindar, Esquire. Another germ for the satire might have been the anonymous *The Ear-Wig; or An Old Woman's Remarks on the Present Exhibition of Pictures of the Royal Academy* which was reviewed by the *Monthly Review* in May, 1781 (384) and was found to be "sprightly but too full of conceits." This prose criticism of the exhibition, judging from the review, merely listed an artist's work and made a general statement—such as bad, poor, or shocking—about it. Another influence might have been the highly complimentary review of the academy's fourteenth annual exhibition in the *London Chronicle* for April 30, 1782 (414). The reviewer found that he couldn't speak about each picture, although "each possesses infinite merit and reflects abundant honour and credit on the respective artists. In short, this year's exhibition is well worthy of the Public, and reflects infinite honour on the Royal Academicians and the Exhibitors, whose several pieces help to make up the show" (414). Such overwhelming praise and recommendation did not coincide with Wolcot's views.

Many of the exhibitors at the Royal Academy are, as a reading of Wolcot's satires reveal, hardly known today. Many of the artists lacked originality and gave an artificial appearance to their subjects and not lifelike qualities. Wolcot's art criticism is quite valid in many respects according to William Sandby, a historian of the Royal Academy;[1] a detailed examination, however, of each ode in a satire would be bulky and unnecessary; therefore, only a few of Peter Pindar's opinions which reveal both his satirical method and his critical stance need be considered.

A summary of Wolcot's views toward the artists merely reiterates the opinions he so clearly, simply, and colloquially expressed in his verses. Briefly, we find that the Royal Academy had, he felt, many inferior artists among its members—artists whose work, in the main, lacked vitality and verisimilitude. Cardboard, wooden, or stonelike figures were passed off on the public by men who painted without observing the true coloring of the landscape and whose portraits and historical paintings revealed a lack of knowledge of anatomy and a lack of respect when dealing with religious subjects. The views on specific artists are just. Time has shown his praise of Richard Wilson, George Stubbs, and Joseph Turner to be valid; and his negative views of painters, with Benjamin West heading the list, agree with subsequent opinion.

As art critic, Pindar advised painters to copy and to follow nature; but portrait painters could allow flattery to guide the brush. Basically, he advocated the use of realism, a view toward life stressed in all his satires. His advice is often ironically given; when serious, he warns against imitating other painters, against attempting to paint in a field such as portraiture when the artist's talent is in landscape painting, and against painting for money if true fame is desired by the artist. The artist must purge himself of envy and jealousy of others and devote his efforts toward self-improvement.

In respect to his poetical style, Wolcot, as will be shown to be the case with his best satires, compares the figure in a painting to an everyday or well-known object: a horse may look like stone; angels, like owls; or figures, like thieves. Illustrative material such as a tale or a story is added to reinforce his points, but such additions are also included merely to lengthen a satire. Wolcot produces his best effects not only through similes but with puns. He apostrophizes the men he satirizes and often presents them as being present and as commenting on the poet. Ferocity in attack is not his method, and good humor (but some occasional bitter irony) pervades the works. The verse forms vary, but iambic pentameter and tetrameter are most prevalent. The heroic couplet is used sparingly; often we find a six-line stanza with rhyme scheme *aabccb*. His verse sentence structure is simple, not convoluted or inverted; and simple words are used which lead to direct, clear statements. With the satires on painters, it can be observed that the humorous effect is primarily achieved through hyperbole, the exaggerated description of what is found in the paintings, such as the repetition of the word *gold* to illustrate the faults of landscape painters.

Another point needs noting. Peter Pindar does not identify the pictures he criticizes; he mentions only the artist's name. This means that his reader saw, or was assumed to have seen, the exhibition; and Wolcot becomes a reporter of a current event in the sense that a gossip columnist is one. If the reader had not seen the exhibition, he could still enjoy most of the satires because of the humorous descriptions of the paintings. But an examination of the satires themselves reveals Wolcot's methods, and he must be quoted so that the flavor of his talents can be obtained.

I Lyric Odes to the Royal Academicians

The fifteen poems, with their varying lines of iambic pentameter and iambic tetrameter which compose *Lyric Odes to the Royal Academicians* (July, 1782), "by Peter Pindar, Esq., a distant Relation of the Poet of Thebes, and Laureate to the Academy," are a mixture of praise, criticism, and advice to painters with occasional overlapping of the three categories. An example of such overlapping appears in "Ode I" in which Sir Joshua Reynolds (1723–92), the academy's president, is praised as being an eagle among wrens; but his *Portrait of an Officer (Col. Tarleton)** is criticized. Peter Pindar objected to the un-lifelike horses which resemble "that Horse/Call'd Trojan, and by Greeks composed of *wood*" (Ode I, 35–36). "Ode IX" expressed the idea that Sir Joshua's imitators abuse art when Peter Pindar declares "I owe Sir Joshua *great*, but Nature *greater*" (1. 19). The copyists err since Sir Joshua is true to nature, which should be the model for painters.

Thomas Gainsborough (1727–88) receives the same treatment given Reynolds. "Ode IV" finds his *Girl with Pigs* worthy only in the depiction of the sow, while his *Portrait of an Officer* (*Major St Leger*) makes the gentleman appear to be a hanged felon. Peter Pindar, who recognized Gainsborough's skill as a landscape painter, offers some criticism and advice at the same time:

> Yet Gainsborough has some merit too,
> Would he his charming *forte* pursue
> To mind his Landscape have the modest grace;

---

*Using the clues which Wolcot gives in his satires, all art works referred to can be located in Algernon Graves, *The Royal Academy of Arts: A Complete Dictionary of Contributors and Their Work from its Foundation in 1769 to 1904* (London, 1906).

> Yet there sometimes are Nature's tints despis'd;
> I wish them more attended to, and priz'd,
> Instead of trumpery that usurps their place.   (Ode IV, 13–18)

"Ode XV" advises George Stubbs (1724–1806), who is highly regarded today as a painter of horses,[2] to continue painting his excellent animal pictures but to discontinue painting human beings. Of the seven works which Stubbs exhibited in 1782, only three were of animals (dogs). "Ode VII" obliquely repeats the advice when the satirist recounts how men, not knowing in what they truly excel, try to achieve fame in some other endeavor. Such a man is Stubbs; he wants to be a landscape painter and "So quits his Horse, on which the man might ride / To Fame's fair temple, happy and unhurt;/ And takes a Hobby-horse to gall his pride" (ll.37–39).

The only artist given complete praise is Richard Wilson (1714–82), who was neglected by his contemporaries but is now considered one of the great English landscape painters.[3] With bitterly ironic lines which reveal Wolcot's low opinion of human nature, he speaks of Wilson's future fame after mentioning the artist's present poverty:

> But, honest Wilson, never mind;
> Immortal praises thou shalt find,
> And for a dinner have no cause to fear.—
> Thou start'st at my prophetic Rhymes:
> Don't be impatient for those times;
> Wait till thou hast been dead a hundred year.
>   (Ode VI, 19–24)

These four—Reynolds, Gainsborough, Stubbs, and Wilson— are the only artists praised; all the others are satirized severely either because of an undignified treatment of a subject or because of an artificial presentation. Benjamin West (1738–1820), the president of the Royal Academy after Reynolds's death and primarily a historical painter, became the prime target for Pindar's views about the inadequate artist. John Rothenstein calls West "a mediocre artist; feeble in imagination and deficient in sense of character, while his colour is monotonous and dry";[4] Miles F. de Montmorency finds West's history pictures to be "academic and lifeless";[5] Grose Evans, however, in *Benjamin West and the Taste of his Times*, (1959) defends West by relating him to his times. Peter Pindar in "Ode II" magnificently roasts West for his picture *The Ascension of our Saviour*. Using a person frequently seen in London for comparison, the satirist particularizes his opinion by saying, "O West, what hath thy pencil done?/Why, painted God Almighty's Son/Like an Old-clothes-Man about London street . . . ? (ll.1–3). West's apostles, he adds, resemble thieves, while his spirits resemble Indian angels. He concedes however, that West must have some merit or he wouldn't be so close to the throne—a glancing reference to George III's artistic taste since the king patronized West.[6]

Mason Chamberlin (d.1787) exhibited three portraits which "Ode VI" claims are wooden figures; and, in the same ode, the four landscapes of Philip James de Loutherbourgh (1740–1812) are found to lack verisimilitude: Loutherbourgh paints "*brass* skies, and *golden* hills,/ With *marble* bullocks in *glass* pastures grazing" 11.8–9). When Richard Cosway (1740–1821) and his wife Maria are examined in "Ode VIII," he is told to find another trade, and she is relegated to such household duties as cooking and sewing. Only vanity, Pindar says, could have prompted them to exhibit their "daubs" which, if Raphael's spirit could examine them, would make him blow the couple's brains out. "Ode X" hopes that Dominic Serres (1722–83) and John Zoffany (1733–1810) will improve with age; and the satire would be evident to those who knew that the former was sixty years old and the latter fifty-nine at the time. George Barret (1728?–84) paints clouds which resemble old rags, while Charles Catton (1728–98) and Edward Penny (1714–91), whose name allows the poet to produce a pun, are numbered among the worst painters of the current exhibition:

> O Catton, our poor feelings spare!
> Suppress thy trash another year;
> Nor of thy folly make us say a hard thing.—
> And, lo! those daubs among the many,
> Painted by Mister Edward *Penny*;
> They truly are not worth half a *farthing*.
>
> (Ode X, 13–18)

These lines reveal one of Wolcot's faults as an artist: he italicizes words so that the reader will not miss a point. Instead of allowing the reader to discover the humor, and thereby see the writer's subtle cleverness, the humor is clearly indicated and the reader sees it and passes over it. Subtlety and its discovery advance the reader's estimation of an artist.

Matthew William Peters (1743–1814) and Angelica Kauffmann (1741–1807) are taken to task in "Ode XII." Peters's *An Angel Carrying the Spirit of a Child to Paradise* has the appearance of a Drury Lane nymph, and the infant soul looks as if it had eaten a hearty meal before the journey. Miss Kauffmann's male figures are insipid, unnatural, and un-alive; she would reject them as partners if such figures actually existed—a touch of the bawdy which may account for Wolcot's success–appealing to a wide reading public. The concluding ode, "Ode XV," gives Nathaniel Hone (1718–84) the unique honor of being the worst painter in the exhibition. Peter Pindar writes, "Of Pictures I have seen enough,/ Most vile, most execrable stuff;/But none so bad as thine, I vow to God" (ll. 10–12).

Peter Pindar's advice to specific artists has already been noted, but he does offer some precepts to painters in general. "Ode II" advises painters to avoid pride, speaks of the necessity of apprenticeship, and mentions the inadvisability of imitating those who paint anything for money. Ironically, in "Ode V," he tells the struggling artist of the benefits derived from a sparse diet since "Fat holds ideas by the legs and wings" (1. 10). The fault of most artists, he claims in "Ode VII," is that they wish to excel in areas not suited to their talents, just as the actor who is superior in farce desires to become a performer in tragedies.

Another piece of gneral advice by Peter Pindar, which is given in "Ode XI," is that one should not follow fashions in painting, since one year the Roman school of Raphael prevails and the next year the Flemish school of Rubens is in the ascendancy. Nature has given everyone eyes, and meant them to be used; "And yet, what thousands, to our vast surprise,/Of Pictures judge by other people's eyes" (ll.21–22).

True representation of figures, realistic depiction of nature, observance of decorum in the treatment of religious subjects, avoidance of following fashions, and faithfulness to a particular area in which one excels are Peter Pindar's strictures to artists. As for the viewer, he should use his native talents—his eyes and common sense—in valuing and judging a picture. Although the pictures exhibited changed each year and new artists emerged, Wolcot still advocated his original points; and, since he did so, his other satires on artists can be dealt with more briefly.

II *Other Lyric Odes to the Royal Academicians*

Pindar's *More Lyric Odes to the Royal Academicians* (July, 1783), composed of eight poems, begins with a series of complaints: his first satire did not sell well, yet the critics were kind; and, though he is thin and hungry, he will retain his critical independence. Using images which he no doubt recalled from his years spent in rural communities, he illustrates the leanness of his physique by contrasting it to Mrs. Cosway's figures in her picture *The Hours,* which is criticized as being unnatural in the process: "No, no; with all my Lyric powers,/I'm not like Mistress Cosway's *Hours,*/ Red as cock-turkeys, plump as barn-door chicken" (ll. 19–21). Only Folly is well fed these days.

In "Ode II" Benjamin West's work is condemned even though nice things can be said about the frames. His *General Monk Receiving King Charles II on the Beach at Dover* makes the king look like a wooden board. *Oliver Cromwell* and *Design for the East Window of St. George's Chapel Windsor; in the Center, the Resurrection; on the Right Hand, St. Peter and St. John; on the Left, the Three Marys* will do to stuff a hole against the wind or to make a window shade. "Ode V" compares the exhibition to Sodom when the poet declares, "Find me ten Pictures in this Exhibition,/That ought not to be damn'd, I'll burn my Odes" (ll. 9–10). Even Sir Joshua Reynolds has lost himself ("Ode VI"), and Richard Cosway has spoiled acres of canvas ("Ode VI").

Peter Pindar's advice in 1783 is far more ironic than that offered in 1782. "Ode VII" illustrates how a painter may become successful by discussing the faults of other artists, thereby increasing his own trade. The artist should paint huge pictures so that each bristle on a pig can be seen from a distance, or he should paint smooth canvases on which brush strokes are not evident, or he should render all trees alike and have them resemble brooms, or "Of Steel and purest Silver form your Waters,/And make your Clouds like Rocks and Alligators" (ll.59–60). The moon should look like a shilling; the sun, like a guinea. The artist should abandon Nature's ways, the satirist advises, and have Nature copy him. Pindar concludes his diatribe in "Ode VIII" by stating that no artist should complain if he hasn't been mentioned. Such a complaint would be regarded as pure impudence and as a desire for any kind of fame when one feels it is "Better be *damn'd,* then mention'd *not at all*" (l.16)!

The *Lyric Odes to the Royal Academicians for the Year 1785* (June, 1785), containing twenty-three poems, opens with a dialogue between "Satire" and the poet. "Satire" asks the poet why he did not attack West in 1784 when five pictures dealing with religious subjects, including two on Moses, were exhibited by that artist. "Satire" claims West's Moses looked like a barber, that the Jews had Christian features, and that West's angels looked more like rocks. Peter replies that he only wished to earn money by his writing and not a libel suit; but he decides to continue his art criticism because "Satire" asks "Where is the *glorious freedom* of our isle,/ If not permitted to call names?" (ll. 42–43). So Benjamin West is examined once again, but not until "Ode V" which finds his *St. Peter's First Sermon after being Filled with the Holy Ghost* to be poorly conceived; St. Peter's coat would make a fine blanket, but the flesh on St. Peter's audience appears to be "Too much like ivory, and stone, and wood" (1. 12). West's *The Lord's Supper* is filled with saints from Tyburn gallows, "With looks so thievish, with such skins of copper!" (1. 17). West's landscape picture is not equal— if such badness were possible—to those of Joseph Wright (1734–97), called Wright of Derby to distinguish him from another painter:

> Thou really does not equal Derby Wright.
> The Man of Night!
> O'er *woolen* hills, where *gold* and *silver* moons
> New mounts like *sixpences*, and now *balloons*;
> Where sea-reflections, nothing *nat'ral* tell ye,
> So much like Fiddle-strings, or Vermicelli:
> Where ev'ry thing exclaimeth, how severe!
> "What *are* we?" and "What bus'ness have we here?"
>
> (ll. 33–40)

Compared with the previous satires, these 1785 *Odes* are more discursive. Wolcot often lengthened a satire by including tales, fables, or stories, and this device could be considered a means to avoid boring the reader with repetitious ideas since many of the inclusions are not too pertinent to the point being made. An example is "Ode VIII" in which the satirist compares saints' relics with the daubs of painters. In France, a church claims to have the thumb of Thomas the Apostle, and this relic is purported to work miracles. The parish's religious inhabitants kiss it frequently and would dismantle it if allowed. Actually, says Peter, the thumb is a painted, rotten stick. This story is then rather poorly applied to painters: certain painters make a daub or a dash to represent eyes, lips, or a nose; fortunately, the British have purer eyes than the French, "So that, whene'er your Figures are *mere wood,*/Our eyes will never deem 'em *flesh and blood*" (ll. 41–42). "Ode X" casts an oblique glance at George III's critical eye when the poet says it is beneficial to the world that monarchs cannot control taste; otherwise, Reynolds would be painting tavern signs.

Wolcot continues to offer painters advice similar to his 1782 and 1783 precepts in his usual lighthearted, ironic manner. "Ode XII" warns artists not to be jealous of one another, for each should try to excel in art instead of in belittling one another. "Ode XIV" indirectly advises painters not to be too swell headed, for the world is inconstant and loves variety; the world is like a group of starlings which alight on horse droppings and then rush off to feast on cow droppings. "Ode XVIII" speaks of the need for education among painters since some prefer to paint a bear or a monkey rather than a sweet girl or would rather paint a stump than a bosom. Landscape painters are told in "Ode XIX" to study nature and not to paint in a garret. There is no art which can make stool legs resemble trees; a pillow, a mountain; a cat, a dog; a bull, a cow. He advises artists to go to Wales for its magnificent scenery and to escape from creditors.

The public, or Peter himself, may have grown weary of these odes, for he offered the academicians fifteen poems in his *Farewell Odes for the Year 1786* (June, 1786). In "Ode X," after declaring that he will no longer write about the academicians, Peter Pindar imaginatively presents the artists as exulting over his announcement. Cautioning them to temper their enthusiasm, he states that, if a person's works may put him in hell, they shall all certainly meet again. As usual, West is quite wittily castigated, in "Ode IV," for his lack of decorum and verisimilitude. West has no notion of what a saint is like:

> And that his cross-wing'd cherubins are Fowls,
> Baptiz'd by naturalists, Owls;
> Half of the meek Apostles, gangs of Robbers;
> His Angels, sets of brazen-headed Lubbers.

(ll. 5–8)

West exhibited two paintings that year which Wolcot refers to in "Ode VIII." *Alexander the Third, King of Scotland, Rescued from the Fury of a Stag* is considered to be an acre of poor painting; and

The Resurrection of Our Saviour makes the poet exclaim "Were our Redeemer like that *wretched thing*?/I do not wonder that the cunning Jews/ Scorn'd to acknowledge *him* for King" (ll. 66–88).

These *Farewell Odes* contain a number of miscellaneous items; "Ode VI," for instance, offers an example of Wolcot's method of expanding a poem when he, to illustrate why one should not despise advice from others, tells a story, "The Pilgrim and the Peas." Two sinners, as penance, are told to walk to a shrine with peas in their shoes. One man is halfway to the shrine when he encounters the other sinner returning from the journey. When the quick-footed sinner is asked how he has fulfilled his penance so rapidly, he replies that he took the liberty of first boiling the peas. This story can refer to the relationship between a painter and a critic if it is annotated, but it is humorous, complete within itself, and could be detached from the *Farewell Odes*. This detachment did occur, for it was later set to music and was illustrated by Thomas Rowlandson, the caricaturist.

Wolcot's advice to painters is still the same. "Ode VII" cautions them not to idolize ancient painters since time has put a coat of varnish over faults for which a modern painter would be attacked. Pindar also ironically advises painters not to praise but to disparage fellow artists; in this way they will receive their commissions. His true opinion, given in "Ode IX," is that he abhors the envy and jealousy among the artists, and he states that a weak painter should acknowledge the superior powers of a better artist. This idea is expanded in "Ode X" where the poet preaches against the vanity of some painters about their own work which is really trash and which should be burned. The public and the artists are told in "Ode XI" that a name should not impose upon judgment since a picture's merits can be traced by the eye. Some respite is given the cardinal principle of following nature in "Ode XII" by requesting the portrait painter to have mercy on a gross-appearing sitter, but the lines also hint that deformity may be a result of dissipation. The conclusion, "Ode XV," offers some consolation to those who do not wish him to discontinue his odes on painting; if the world requests more, the poet will give it what it desires.

Although *Subjects for Painters* (June, 1789) does not deal with artists specifically but with political matters, the satire does contain material referring to this subject. The prose preface addressed to the reader speaks of the current rage for historical pictures, a reference

is made to John Boydell (1719–1804) and his Shakespeare Gallery,
an exhibition of painting illustrating scenes from Shakespeare's
plays. Peter Pindar hopes that, when Shakespeare and Milton are
exhausted as subjects, the artists will illustrate the suggestions
offered in the miscellaneous work which follows. He tells the academicians that he comes in peace, that he is not going to attack them,
but in the same breath he actually does so:

> O West! that fix'd and jealous eye forbear,
> Which scowling marks the Bard with doubt and fear;
>   Thy Forms are sacred from my wrath divine:
> 'Twere *cruel* to attack such crippled creatures,
> So very, very feeble in their natures,
>   Already gasping in a deep *decline*.
>
>   (ll.47–52)

> Nor come I here t'inform some men so wise,
>   Who shine not yet upon the R. A. list,
> That Limbs in Spasms and *crack'd*, and *goggling Eyes*,
>   With Grandeur cannot well exist.
> Nay, let it be recorded in my Rhyme,
> Convulsions cannot give the true Sublime.
>
>   (ll.75–80)

> No, Landscape-painters: let your *gold* streams sleep;
>   Sleep *golden* skies and bulls, and *golden* cows,
> And *golden* groves and vales, and *golden* sheep,
>   And *golden* goats, the *golden* grass that brouse;
>
> With which such *golden* lustre flame,
> As beat the very *golden* frame!
>
>   (ll.87–92)

The poet then imagines that Benjamin West is attacking his verse,
calling it a poor rushlight and not truth's torch. Peter says that no
matter what is said, he will continue to give advice; and what follows
are topics—presented in odes, tales, and lyrics—which the painters
may use for subject matter.

A few minor references to the Royal Academy are found in the
satirist's work prior to the last satire on this group in 1808. *The
Rights of Kings; or Loyal Odes to Disloyal Academicians* (June,
1791), though its inception was the refusal of the academy to select

Thomas Lawrence, the King's choice, as a member of the body,[7] does not deal with painters per se; it is a satire on the king and his lost prerogatives although it advises painters to regain royal favor by becoming completely acquiescent to the king's wishes. When Joshua Reynolds died in 1782, Benjamin West became the academy's president, and Peter Pindar wrote "Ode to the Academic Chair, on the Election of Mr. West to the Presidency," which appeared as one of the *Odes of Importance* (June, 1792). Here the satirist deals with the new president as he dealt with Sir Joseph Banks, president of the Royal Society; namely, that it is a disgrace for such a man to occupy the position. "How art thou fallen, thou *once* high-honour'd Chair" (1.1), begins the poem, to be occupied by a man who is as "full of wisdom as an egg of meat!" (1. 44). The King admires West's pictures, and West admires the King's taste—a strange turn of events since Reynolds felt that George III knew nothing about art. Well, the poet concludes, the elevation of West proves that people with very little can still be blessed.

Celebration, or the Academic Procession to St. James's (February, 1794) is similar to *The Rights of Kings* in that it it deals with the king and not with painters. Its "Advertisement to the Reader" merely mentions how the academy has knuckled under to the king's veto of certain measures, and then it deals with submission and loyalty to the king in an ironic manner.

Wolcot's last satire addressed to and devoted to the academicians appeared late in his life and may have been an attempt to recapture his dwindling audience by returning to an earlier, successful theme. *One More Peep at the Royal Academy* (April, 1808) is a repetition of the satirist's old ideas which are applied primarily to new painters although some of his older subjects for ridicule are still mentioned. The poem entitled "West" states that his *The Death of Lord Nelson in the Cockpit of the Ship* will do since the hero's form has not been disgraced; however, his two paintings based on mythology are criticized, but in a mellow manner and tone:

> West, let me as a friend advise:
> From classic ground withdraw thine eyes,
> Nor fancy from *sublime* to gather glory,
> Attempt not things beyond thy reach:
> The Pebble on the sandy beach,
> Can ne'er expect to rise a Promontory.

(ll. 37–42)

In "Fuseli," Henry Fuseli (1741–1825) is told that his portrait of Beaufort is ill constructed and "Thy *blue* and *green flesh* (let me say)/No *compliment* to Beauty pay:/A *putrid carcass* is not *charming nature*" (ll. 46–48). If Fuseli painted God as a man of war, he would "Cut down the Thunderer to a *privateer*" (1. 84). Furthermore, Pindar discovers in "Loutherbourg" that his advice on landscape painting has not been heeded; but then, the world likes glare. Singled out for praise are John Lane (1788–1868), David Wilke (1785–1841), and Joseph Mallord William Turner (1775–1851); and the last artist is called the best of the group, for nature gave Turner a giant's brain.

The major portion of *One More Peep* is devoted to "Odes to the Heads," an anonymous entry, and the heads are called "melancholy sad burlesques on Nature" (1. 6). The heads are attacked because they are of members of the lower class and do not exhibit any grace in physical features. The "Conclusion" once again finds the bulk of the exhibited work lacking in quality:

> Now to be *serious*, O ye men!
> (Few Eagles, and too many a Wren,)
> How dare ye fill the room with such *pollution*?
> Will Justice say, while thus ye *hang*
> So sad and villainous a gang,
> *Yourselves* should not be led to *execution*?
>
> (ll.1–6)

Peter Pindar feels that the works of genius and those of real merit have been omitted; and he closes by advising George III himself, or by his command to the porter, to knock the exhibitors' heads together.

III   Peter Pindar's Art Principles

This examination of Wolcot's art criticism reveals that he follows typical neoclassical standards: imitate nature, observe decorum, use common sense, and so forth. These easy-to-grasp strictures, plus his conversational and iconoclastic method, may account for his early popularity. Essentially, Wolcot's appeal lies in his straightforward approach with its absence of technical terms, a method which enabled any person who could read to grasp his meaning. Furthermore, his satires are written with a good-natured grace, a lack of rancor, and touches of irony. The tone is not that of a shrill, hoarse scream of abuse; it is like a gentle chuckle over foolishness or ineptitude. Thus, painters are fools when they do not follow reason and nature, and the public is foolish when it pays homage to a name and does not trust its own eyes.

As an impressionistic critic of art, Peter Pindar did not write rules by which a painting could be judged, nor did he present specific, constructive advice for painters to follow. Rather, he offered general precepts, such as following nature, which were familiar to his contemporaries; and these precepts were placed in verse whereby the works of well-known painters were shown to be lacking in execution and realism. This means that Wolcot was first of all a satirist, and second, an art critic; his impressions on art may have been sound, but this was not his primary purpose in writing. Because of the genial humor of this reporter, this gossip columnist, he was read— and also because of that strange element in human nature which delights in the deflation of an honored public personality.

CHAPTER 3

Satires on Literary Figures

A FTER successfully and profitably attacking the Royal Academy
in four poems (1782, 1783, 1785, 1786) and after completing
Canto I (1786) of *The Lousiad,* a satire directed against George III,
John Wolcot found a perfect object for ridicule in James Boswell's
Journal of a Tour to the Hebrides with Samuel Johnson, LL.D.
(1785). Literary figures and specific works were now to be examined
by Pindar; and James Boswell, Thomas Warton, Henry James Pye,
James Bruce, and Hannah More each received one or more pamphlets devoted to them with an occasional reference in other poems.
As with the satires on the Royal Academicians, Peter Pindar's
literary standards of judgment, direct and indirect, are seen as
examples of neoclassic norms.

In these satires, John Wolcot utilizes, primarily, the manner of
Horace in attacking human foibles and the content of the works
under observation. He does not rant, rave, or sadistically slash his
victims; instead, he is urbane, stands somewhat at a distance, and
speaks with a mocking smile upon his face. He questions the meaning and value of each work, and the basic standard which he indirectly measures his victims against is truth. He stresses that
veracity, common sense, and decorum must be observed by a writer;
undeserving flattery of the great, egotism, and bias should not be
aspects of a writer's personality. James Boswell is attacked for his
egotism, his rather unflattering anecdotes of Dr. Johnson, and only
indirectly for his style. Warton and Pye, the poet laureates, are
charged with gross flattery of the king, thus allowing Peter Pindar
opportunity to attack the petty pursuits of George III. James Bruce
is viewed as another Boswell, an egotistical braggart; but Bruce has
the added distinction of being called a liar who fabricates out-
rageous stories concerning the wonders of nature. Miss More's
writings, and particularly her style, are considered to be involved,
weighty, dull, and devoid of lasting qualities. But Bishop Porteus's
eulogy on an inferior work arouses the satirist's view of the human
mind led astray from reason and common sense; and Miss More's
piety and self-righteousness are called into question.

Of Wolcot's techniques here, the mock encomium—verse sentences for Bruce and Boswell, brief adjectives for the others—is the primary satiric method. Once again the comparison of people to animals is used as is the disabling adjective and the exaggerated example. He utilizes the victim's own works—Wolcot again being a reporter—which, through quotation and commentary, reveal vanity and folly. Arguing for moderation and proportion, while indirectly asking his reader to use common sense, Peter Pindar presents himself as a sane judge of society and of literature; and he expresses views of his victims shared by many of his contemporaries.

I British Biographers

When Boswell's *Journal of a Tour* was published, the *Gentleman's Magazine* for November, 1785 (889–94) called it an entertaining and instructive work; but the satirist disagreed. Unable to tolerate Boswell's egotism, his name dropping, and his reporting of minutiae, John Wolcot produced *A Poetical and Congratulatory Epistle to James Boswell, Esq., on His Journal of a Tour to the Hebrides with the Celebrated Dr. Johnson* (April, 1786). In the form of formal verse satire, Boswell is directly addressed and is seen as ambitious for fame, an aspect of madness:

> O Boswell, Bozzy, Bruce, whate'er thy name,
> Thou mighty Shark for anecdote and fame;
> Thou Jackall, leading Lion Johnson forth
> To eat Macpherson 'midst his native North;
> To frighten grave professors with his roar,
> And shake the Hebrides from shore to shore:
> All Hail!—At length, ambitious Thane, thy rage
> To give one spark to Fame's bespangled page,
> Is amply gratified:—a thousand eyes
> Survey thy books with rapture and surprise.
> Loud, of thy Tour, a thousand tongues have spoken,
> And wondered that thy bones were never broken.   (ll.1–12)

After this ironic beginning, which illustrates the author's characteristic short, biting metaphors and his use of anticlimax, the reader is given a series of footnoted references in heroic couplets to Boswell's *Journal of a Tour* to enforce the idea that "Bozzy" has given the reading public a mass of anecdotes devoid of importance and, at times, unflattering to Dr. Johnson. After a number of references

to Boswell's descriptions of Dr. Johnson's clothes and personal
habits Peter Pindar gives an anticlimactic thrust to some lines of
mock praise:

> Rare Anecdotes! 'tis Anecdotes like these
> That bring thee glory, and the Million please:
> On these shall future times delighted stare,
> Thou charming Haberdasher of Small Ware.   (ll.111–14)

Since Sir John Hawkins and Madam Piozzi are each planning
to write a life of Johnson, the satirist pretends to see nothing in-
congrous in the fact that Boswell should also plan one. Using one
of his favorite devices, comparison of persons to animals, Peter
Pindar presents a picture of Boswell's catlike working methods:

> Then why not thou each joke and tale enrol,
> Who, like a watchful Cat before a hole,
> Full twenty years (inflam'd with letter'd pride)
> Didst *mousing* sit before Sam's mouth so wide
> To catch as many scraps as thou wert able,
> A very Lazarus at the rich man's table?   (ll.205–10)

Commentary about Boswell's abuse of friendship and about his
qualifications as a Johnson biographer is followed by advising
Boswell to invent more anecdotes or to search for them in Bolt
Court where Dr. Johnson lodged, anecdotes which could serve
as the basis for the future biography. Boswell should tell the world,
Peter suggests, of Johnson's eating, sneezing, coughing, and "On
tales, however strange, impose thy claw" (1. 299). In the conclusion
to this verse epistle, Boswell is told that he is merely a cracker
attached to the tail of comet Johnson.

The prose postscript to the poem relates of an imaginary visit—a
favorite device skillfully used by Wolcot—to Johnson's lodgings
by the satirist a few months before the doctor's death, a visit during
which Boswell is indirectly requested by Johnson to reconsider his
plans for becoming his biographer. Peter Pindar states that Boswell
is contemplating a biography of the lexicographer; and Johnson's
response, as written by Wolcot, is a happy and fitting parody of
Boswell's presentation of Johnson's manner and style. Dr. Johnson
says, "Sir, he cannot mean me so irreparable an injury. Which
of us shall die first, is only known to the Great Disposer of events;
but were I sure that James Boswell would write *my* Life, I do not

know whether I would not anticipate the measure by taking *his*."
Assured that Boswell does plan to do so, Johnson in righteous
wrath replies: "Boswell write my life! why the fellow possesses not
abilities for writing the life of an *ephemeron*."

Perhaps the subject of Boswell and Johnson would have been
dropped at this point if Mrs. Piozzi had not published her *Anecdotes
of the Late Doctor Johnson* (1786). Mrs. Piozzi's anecdotes were
regarded as a defamation of Johnson's character, and the *Monthly
Review* for April, 1786, sarcastically observed that "Johnson's
enemies judiciously left the office of *biographer* to his friends"
(373). In a letter to Horace Mann, dated March 28, 1786, Horace
Walpole wrote that, though Mrs. Piozzi praises the doctor, "almost
every fact she relates disgraces him."[1] Continuing the letter the
next day, Walpole remarked, "There is a Dr. Wolcot, a burlesque
bard, who had ridiculed highly, and most deservedly, another of
Johnson's biographic zanies, one Boswell; he has already adver-
tised an ecologue to be published next week; and indeed, there is
ample matter."[2]

Bozzi and Piozzi; or The British Biographers. A Town Ecologue
(1786) went through ten editions in two years;[3] George Saintsbury
refers to it as "the best thing of its particlar kind ever written."[4]
The satire presents Mrs. Piozzi and James Boswell as if each were
contending for the position of Johnson's biographer. Since neither
knew "*Which* bore the palm of Anecdote away" (1.62), they agree
to have Sir John Hawkins (who would soon publish his own biography of Johnson) sit in judgment upon their little known facts.
What follows is a series of footnoted anecdotes alternately given
by each contestant for "the palm of Anecdote." Two examples
give the reader an adequate idea of the meaningless anecdotes
related. Boswell, drawing his material from the tour to the Hebrides,
reveals:

> While Johnson was in Edinburgh, my Wife,
> To please his palate, studied for her life:
> With every rarity she fill'd her house,
> And gave the Doctor, for his dinner, grouse.   (ll.105–8)

Madame Piozzi's reply is equally full of meaning and importance:

> Dear Doctor Johnson was in size an Ox:
> And from his uncle Andrew learn'd to *box*:
> A man to Wrestlers and to Bruisers dear,
> Who kept the ring in Smithfield a whole year.   (ll.109–12)

The numerous scraps of information descend upon the ears of Sir John Hawkins with such a furious pace that he bids the anecdotists stop while he refreshes himself with a nap. In a dream, Johnson appears to give Hawkins some advice:

> "Wake, Hawkins," growled the Doctor with a frown,
> "And knock that Fellow and that Woman down,
> Bid them with Johnson's Life proceed no further:
> Enough already have they dealt in murther.
> Say, to their tales that little truth belongs:
> If *fame* they mean me, bid them *hold their tongues*."   (II, ll. 5–10)

After Hawkins awakes, he unwisely allows the two anecdotists to continue. Realizing his mistake after listening to more interminable accounts of minor matters, Hawkins cries "Shame" and informs the pair they have slandered Johnson. Unable to decide which is the worse slanderer, Sir John tells Madame Piozzi to return to her duties as a wife and requests Boswell to discontinue his egotisms and pretensions and never leave Scotland again. The poem concludes with Hawkins hurrying off to collect anecdotes for his own biography of Johnson, and "The Rivals marvelling mark'd his sudden flight;/ Then to their pens and paper rush'd the twain,/ To *kill* the mangled Rambler o'er *again*" (ll. 382–84).

These two works are the main attacks on Boswell, but *A Benevolent Epistle to Sylvanus Urban, Alias Master John Nichols* (June, 1970) contains two references to Bozzy who "High-panting for the echo of a name,/ Should meanly crucify poor Johnson's fame" (ll. 177–78). The text reference pertains, no doubt, to the May, 1786, review of Wolcot's *Epistle to James Boswell* in Sylvanus Urban's (John Nichols's) *Gentleman's Magazine* which stated that Boswell's *Journal of a Tour* would be read and admired while people would slumber over the satirist's poem (416). Using the usual defense of the satirist, Peter Pindar claims he attacks only folly and lack of reason:

> Vex'd that the Muse (as if she utter'd treason)
> Should try to bring poor Boswell back to reason;
> (Herculean toil, to keep such folly under!)
> Loud from thy head's dark Cloud I felt thy Thunder.   (ll. 215–18)

James Bruce's *Travels to Discover the Source of the Nile* was published also in 1790, and it gave Wolcot another opportunity to attack Boswell. Viewing both Boswell and Bruce as proud, egotistical collectors of trivia, the satirist compared and damned both figures with mock praise in the prose epistle preceding the satire in heroic couplets, *A Complimentary Epistle to James Bruce, Esq., The Abyssinian Traveler* (October, 1790). Addressing Bruce, he writes, in part:

What a similarity, illustrious Sir, between yourself and Mr. James Boswell; and yet what a distance! both gloriously ambitious, both great Scholars, both intellectually adorned, both popular Gentlemen, both Dealers in History, and both descended from Kings. But Mr. James Boswell's Ambition was not of so bold a wing as yours. *He* was content with a journey to Scotland, to exhibit Dr. Samuel Johnson, the lexicographer, to the *literati* of that country: *your* more exalted ideas could only be satisfied with a display of the Head-quarters of the immortal Nile, who had puzzled the pursuits of men for seven thousand years. While Mr. Boswell entertains only with a breakfast on Spaldings (*alias* dried Whitings), the Sublimer Bruce treats us with a Dish of Lion. While Boswell brings us acquainted with plain Scottish gentlewomen only, the gallant Bruce charms us with romantic tales of Queen Sittinia, etc.

The "Ode to Lord Lonsdale," one of the *Odes of Importance* (June, 1792), also refers to Boswell's tour to the Hebrides. Speaking of a camel that carried a grinning monkey, the satirist is reminded of Doctor Johnson "ponderous moving through the Northern track,/ With dapper Jemmy Boswell on his back" (ll. 41–42). The last reference by Wolcot to James Boswell occurs in "Sir Joshua Reynolds" found in *Pindariana* (1794) when the satirist repeats the rumor that Boswell is planning a life of Reynolds. Johnson is pictured as rising from the grave and as bidding Boswell not to murder another man with biography.

II The Poet Laureates

Following Wolcot's success with Boswell in 1786, he aimed his verses at Thomas Warton (1728–90), the poet laureate, who was to make his laureate odes "the plaything of his antiquarian and romantic ideas."[5] Warton was an acknowledged poet who had been professor of poetry at Pembroke College and was Camden professor of History at Oxford at the time of his appointment in April, 1785.[6] Unluckily for Warton, Peter Pindar could not allow flattery unconnected with reality to go unnoticed, especially if it referred to George III. Thomas Warton's "New Year's Ode for 1787" contained a brief historical survey of the function of the poet toward his king. He began with the minstrel and brought the survey to the present day where the poet "moulds his harp to manners mild" (1. 36); sings of kings "Diffusing commerce, peace and art" (1. 42); and, Warton concludes, sings:

> To Kings who rule a filial land,
> Who claim a people's vows and pray'rs,
> Should Treason arm the weakest hand:
> To these his heart-felt praise he bears,
>   And with new rapture hastes to greet
>   This festal morn, that longs to meet,
>   With luckiest auspices, the laughing spring:
> And opes her glad career with blessings on her wing.

This rather muted praise of the king and perhaps the success of the satire by many hands called *Probationary Odes for the Laureatship* (1785) led to Peter Pindar's *Ode Upon Ode* (March, 1787) which the author called an amplification of Warton's ode. The "Proemium" offers advice to anyone who may become the court's "Lyric Trumpeter" (1. 13):

> Whene'er employ'd to celebrate a King,
> Let *Fancy* lend thy Muse her loftiest wing;
>   Stun with thy minstrelsy th' affrighted sphere:
> Bid thy Voice like a hundred Batteries;
> For *common* sounds, conveying *common* flatteries
>   Are Zephyrs whisp'ring to the Royal ear.   (ll.17–22)

In the ode itself, the minstrels of ancient times are mentioned; but now, according to Warton, says Peter, poets have a worthier subject:

> The Poet "moulds his harp to manners mild,"
> (Quoth Tom) to Monarchs who, with rapture wild,
> Hear their *own* Praise with mouths of gaping Wonder,
> And catch each crotchet of the Birth-day Thunder: (ll.45–48)

After a thrust at the critical abilities of the court circle which had warmly received the laureate's ode, Peter Pindar returns to the "New Year's Ode for 1787" and claims that the modern poet must now sing of economy-minded kings, of commercial treaties, of taxes, and of excisemen. The "Conclusion" finds the satirist un-envious of Warton's numbers and of the laureate's place; if he were offered the post, he would decline on the grounds of an in-ability to write fiction. Defending this attack in *An Apologetic Postscript to Ode Upon Ode* (June 1787), Wolcot based his argument upon economic grounds. If he wrote of common folks, no one would buy his rhymes; and this lack of sale would cause him great distress since he likes to eat. Furthermore, no one should object to the verses since he is recording history and, in addition, wishes to reform the court.

Thomas Warton's "Ode on His Majesty's Birth-day, June 4th, 1787" contained more overt praise than his "New Year's Ode." After mentioning Chaucer, Edmund Spenser, and John Dryden, Warton claimed:

> Had these blest bards been call'd to pay
> The vows of this auspicious day,
> Each had confess'd a fairer throne,
> A mightier sovereign than his own!   (ll. 49–52)

Warton's panegyric sharpened Wolcot's wits and he produced *Instructions to a Celebrated Laureat* (August, 1787) which asked: "Yet, 'midst thy heap of compliments so fine,/ Say, may we venture to *believe* a line?/ You Oxford Wits most dearly love a *joke*" (ll. 4–6). The poet laureate is told that Spenser and even Dryden had better sovereigns to write about, and he is requested to put down only the truth. To impregnate the lesson, Peter Pindar intends to teach the laureate his craft; and he pens a "Birthday Ode" which begins:

> This day, this very day, gave birth,
> *Not* to the *brightest* Monarch upon earth,
>   *Because* there are *some* brighter, and as big;
> Who love the Arts that Man exalt to Heaven:
> George loves them also, when they're giv'n
>   To four-legg'd Gentry, christened Dog and Pig,
> Whose deeds in our wonder-hunting Nation
> Prove what a charming thing is *education*.   (ll. 1–8)

After this ridicule of the king's pleasure in viewing dancing dogs and wise pigs, the satirist portrays what George III actually did on his birthday: the monarch had visited Whitebread's brewery and had learned the art of brewing beer. The laureate is told that the way to write a birthday ode has been demonstrated; he is to stick to the truth and is not to praise kings for imaginary qualities.

Warton's "Ode for the New Year, 1788" historically surveyed times when Britain was in danger of foreign invasion and did not mention the king at all, probably because of the sovereign's mental illness at the time.[7] So, in *Brother Peter to Brother Tom* (April, 1788), Peter wondered why the laureate was silent and conjectured that Warton might have lost the art of invention or perhaps wanted to be relieved of his duties:

> With pity I have seen thee, Son of Song,
> Thrundling thy Lyric Wheelbarrow along,
> Amidst Saint James's gapers to unload
> The motley mass of pompour Ode:
> And wish'd the Sack, for Verse the annual prize,
> To poets of less renown—   (ll. 569–74)

When Thomas Warton died on May 20, 1790, Peter offered some instruction to his then unknown successor in *Advice to the Future Laureat* (August, 1790). Pretending an eager desire to see the future laureate, the poet pictures the rush of candidates for the office, including among them William Mason (1724–97), the poet and biographer of Thomas Gray, and William Hayley (1745–1820), the poet and biographer of William Cowper:

> Dread Rivals, splashing through the dirty road,
> With thundering Specimens of Ode;
> The Lyric bundles on each Poet's back,
> Intent to gain the Stipend and the Sack;
> See Mason, Hayley, to the Palace scamper,
> Like Porters sweating underneath a hamper!
> And see the Hacks of Nichols' Magazine
> Rush loyal to berhyme a King and Queen: (ll. 5–12)

Pindar warns the future laureate that he will have to write of animals on the king's farm and of royal economy and not act as did Warton, a scholar, who believed books were read at court. If Pindar were king, he would appoint no laureate but would make the court a place for science, art, and distinguished men and not, as it presently is, a haven for small minds.

Following a complimentary review of Pindar's *Advice to the*

Future Laureat, the *Monthly Review* for August, 1790, added a few lines on the post of poet laureat to show that it agreed with the satirist's views: "Indeed, it was always a matter of surprize to us, to see men of real talents, and truly respectable for literary character, condescending to place on their brows a wreath of laurel, bestowed on such terms, as it might be imagined would allure none but a Shadwell, a Tate, a Eusden, or a Cibber" (449).

Unfortunately, Wolcot's wish for no appointment to poet laureate was not granted, for the post was given in July, 1790, to Henry James Pye (1745–1813), a man who is acknowledged by those who mention him to have been a poor choice and a feeble poet.[8] Kenneth Hopkins regards him an amateur who "year by year affirmed with real sincerity that there never was a king like George."[9] W. Forbes Gray found Pye to be the worst of the laureates whose verses for twenty-two years contained "gross adulation, sheer impudence, and poetic worthlessness,"[20] and Edmund Kemper Broadus dismissed Pye as being dull and inept.[11] John Wolcot did not devote an entire poem to Pye until 1795, possibly because there was no need to comment on flattery so outrageously obvious or because of his own involvement with such larger game as John Nichols and Thomas Paine; but Pye was briefly mentioned in other works.

In *The Remonstrance* (October, 1791), while denying that he has joined the court just because he attacked Thomas Paine, Peter Pindar states he has never praised the court; and he adds a few damning lines on the post of poet laureate and Pye, a beast of burden, "Who trotteth, with a grave and goodly pace,/ Deep-laden with his Sovereign, twice a year" (ll. 88–89):

> Court Poets must *create*, on *trifles* rant.
> Make *something* out of *nothing*; Lord I can't!
> Bards must bid Virtues crowd on Kings in *swarms*,
>   However from such company *remote*; (ll.99–102)

More Money (February, 1792) briefly uses Pye as an example in economy by pointing out he published only a birthday ode and not a New Year's ode that year.

The poem actually dedicated by Pindar to Pye, *The Royal Tour, and Weymouth Amusements: A Solemn and Reprimanding Epistle to the Laureate* (November, 1795), is used to exhibit the foibles of the king even though Pye does have his share of criticism. In the prose letter preceding the poem, Pye is reprimanded for writing only one ode a year when everything that is said, done, or conceived by the king is worthy of recording. Then Peter Pindar records the little doings of the king—staring at bullocks, pigs, and fish—and he wonders how Pye can sleep when such things are happening. He recommends that Pye follow the king about so that all these wonderful events can be preserved for posterity.

Pye is also referred to in two other poems. *The Convention Bill* (December, 1795), which deals with the precarious state of affairs for writers in England during the period of the wars with France, manages to attack the bill's proposed censorship, Pye, and the king in two lines of the "Ode to Mr. Pitt": "Thus let *our* Caesar mounted be on high,/ And no one *take his name in vain* but Pye" (ll. 49–50). The last entry on Pye occurs in an "Elegy,"[12] one of the miscellaneous pieces which compose *Tristia* (December, 1806). The poet merely mentions that he never wished to destroy the throne; he only sought the social equality of drinking sack with Laureate Pye.

III   Travelers

When James Bruce (1730–94) returned from his Abyssinian travels to England in 1774, he waited sixteen years before publishing his *Travels to Discover the Source of the Nile, in the Years 1768, 1769, 1770, 1771, 1772, 1773* in five volumes. On his return to England, however, he did relate a number of incidents which occurred on his journey; and they were regarded as inventions of an imaginative mind. On Sunday, October 14, 1787, Horace Walpole wrote to Hannah More, "Bruce is printing his travels, which I suppose will prove that his narratives were fabulous, as he will scarce repeat them by the press."[13]

When the *Monthly Review* examined the volumes in June, July, August, and October of 1790, it found much to disparage. The *Travels* were discovered to be too lengthy as a result of repetitious statements; furthermore, the narrative's authenticity was also questioned. It was reported that Mr. Bruce's "maps do not correspond with the text, whose drawings differ from his descriptions, whose citations from Greek writers do not authenticate the facts for which they are adduced, and whose own narrative is often inconsistent and some times contradictory" (June, 1790, 186). Bruce's praise of himself as an expert on language, manners, navigation, business, and shooting is mocked by merely listing his accomplishments (189).

The review (continued in the July, August, and October issues) is a synopsis of the *Travels*, and the conclusion in the October, 1790, issue repeated the earlier statements about exaggerated, inconsistent, and contradictory material. Wolcot's *A Complimentary Epistle to James Bruce* received a favorable review in the same October, 1790, issue (219–20), and the reviewer hinted that the readers of Bruce's *Travels* would agree with Peter's views on the subject. It should be stated, however, that, though Bruce did not discover the source of the Nile, his "truthfulness has been sufficiently established", and his book, according to Richard Garnett, will remain "the epic of African travel."[14]

Wolcot's attack on Bruce again reveals the satirist as a reporter in verse; anyone currently being discussed by the public and the periodicals could become a satiric victim. If, in his view, the individual received unwarranted praise, as was the case with Hannah More, he expressed his supposedly correct assessment. If the individual was disparaged, as was Bruce, he attacked his subject's pride and his lack of moderation and common sense. Of course, Wolcot did not satirize all prominent figures disparaged or praised by the public or the press; those he attacked had to possess failings which he felt needed correction. So Wolcot continues to express wonderment at man's credulity, his self-aggrandizement, and his self-deception.

As previously noted, Peter Pindar's prose "Epistle Dedicatory" to the *Epistle to James Bruce* compares the traveler to James Boswell and finds him superior to the anecdotist in pride and in egotism, and as a narrator of superfluous information. The "Complimentary Epistle" itself regards the *Travels* as a piece of fabrication which the public, delighted with anything new, will happily read: 'Sweet is the Tale, howe'er uncouth its shape,/ That makes the World's wide mouth with Wonder gape" (ll. 3–4). Man's curiosity bids him seek fame by searching for wonders in strange places, but Bruce is most fortunate because nature wants to display her wonders to him, a sign of Bruce's vivid imagination:

> Lo! moon-eyed Wonder opes her lap, to thee:
> How *niggardly*, alas, to *luckless* me!
> Where'er through trackless woods thy *luckier* way,
> Marvels, like Dew-drops, beam on ev'ry spray.
> Blest Man! whate'er thou *wishest* to behold,
> Nature as strongly *wishes* to unfold:

> Of all her Wardrobes offers every Rag,
> Of which thy skill hath form'd a Conjuror's Bag.
>
> (ll.99–106)

Peter envies Bruce because he, the satirist, neither saw nor discovered any marvels in the West Indies: "Whate'er *I* saw, requir'd no Witch's Storm;/ Slight deeds, that *Nature* could with ease perform" (ll. 187–88). No, nothing spectacular had occurred or had appeared for Peter; no eagle had stolen meat from him, nor had a crocodile observed him, and he had never eaten a lion. Bruce, however, saw wonders everywhere, for the sky seemed to rain them upon him. Ironically, Peter suggests that Bruce was modest and concealed much information:

> I fear thou hidest *half* thy feats, unkind;
> A thousand wonders, ah! remain behind.
> Where is the *chariot-wheel* with *Pharoah's name*,
> Fish'd from the old *Red-Sea* to swell thy fame?
> Where wicked Pharoah and his host were drown'd?
> Where of that *stone* a *slice*, and fresh account,
> Given by the Lord to Moses on the *Mount*?   (ll.259–66)

Pindar bids this "Sagacious Terrior in Discovery's mine" (l. 275) not to heed the criticism which questioned the authenticity of his narratives; Bruce should return to the Nile region, find new wonders, return with new treasures, plus new books, "And mind ('tis History's province to *surprise*),/ That Tales are *sweetest*, that *sound most like lies*" (ll. 339–40).

This advice concludes the main epistle, but Peter Pindar added that Bruce is so superior to Boswell that he earned an "Ode to James Bruce, Esq." In it, Peter repeats his advice: Bruce should ignore the critics and return to Abyssinia to collect more tales and artifacts. This added poem is so similar in thought and expression to the main verse epistle that it can only be considered as material to add bulk to a slim pamphlet.

IV   Blue Stockings

Perhaps the most ungentlemanly satire Peter Pindar ever wrote was the one directed against Hannah More (1745–1833) in 1799. Since she was a member of the "blue stocking" society—a term to describe that literary group of ladies and gentlemen amply treated in Miss More's poem *Bas Bleu* (1786)—the female "blues" also received a few lashes from the satirist's whip. Although an entire poem directed to her did not appear until 1799, she is mentioned in Wolcot's earliest work of professional polish, *A Poetical, Supplicating, Modest, and Affecting Epistle to those Literary Colossuses, the Reviewers* (August, 1778). As might be expected, the poem attacks the reviewers' poor taste and, in particular, their views about Hannah More. By 1778, Hannah More had achieved some literary fame with three dramas in verse: *The Search for Happiness* (1762), *The Inflexible Captive* (1774), and the tragedy *Percy* (1777).

The reviewer in May, 1774, issue of the *Gentleman's Magazine* (225) was pleased to report that the pastoral drama, *The Search for Happiness*, was now in its third edition. In this drama, four young ladies—Euphelia, Cleona, Pastorella, and Laurinda—after relating their inability to discover happiness at court, in society, or in the works of literature, are told by Urania, an old shepherdess, "that the chief happiness and misery of mortals are owing to a good or bad education" (225); and Urania advises them to study wisdom, virtue, and religion. The reviewer then recommends the book to young female readers. *Percy*, as reviewed in the *Gentleman's Magazine*, January, 1778 (33–34), is a rather involved, melodramatic tale of love and jealousy in which Elwina's scarf serves the same function as Desdemona's handkerchief in *Othello*, though the conclusion seems an echo of *Hamlet*. In a duel, Earl Douglas stabs Percy, Elwena's former lover; Elwena accidentally swallows poison; and Earl Douglas, her husband, stabs himself. The anonymous reviewer stated that this drama of pathos and sensibility, whose language is "correct, animated, and nervous" (34), received deserved applause.

This type of praise rankled Peter Pindar's sense of correctness; and in *Epistle to the Reviewers*, while mockingly praising the reviewers' integrity, he condemns their judgment:

> "Could Gold succeed, enough the Peer might raise,
>   Whose wealth would buy the Critics o'er and o'er;
> 'Tis merit only can command their praise;
>   Witness the volumes of Miss Hannah More:

> "The *Search for Happiness*, that beauteous Song
>   Which all of us would give our ears to own;

> The *Captive, Percy,* that, like mustard strong,
> Make our eyes weep, and understandings groan."

(ll.81–88)

In Canto I (1786) of *The Lousiad,* a reference is made to Miss More's *Sacred Dramas* (1782), a work which M. G. Jones, one of Miss More's biographers, refers to as containing "stiff wooden verses of formal gravity."[15] In Pindar's satire dealing with the discovery of a louse upon the king's plate during the dinner hour, he speaks of trifling interior matter of the brain and, for an example, asks the reader to witness the "Sacred Dramas of Miss Hannah More,/Where all the Nine with little Moses snore" (ll. 421–22). Miss More and the literary ladies of the "Bas Bleu" are mentioned in the "Elegy to Apollo," found in *A Benevolent Epistle to Sylvanus Urban* (1787), in which the poet complains of the cruelty of other writers toward his verse:

> I see the band of Blue Stockings arise,
>   Historic, critic, and poetic Dames:
> This lifts her palms, and that her marvelling eyes;
>   And squeaks, "The fellow's stuff should feel the flames;
>
> Such is the Way his works should come to *light.*"
>   Thus rail those Dames of classic Erudition;
> Thus leagued with Wit, unmerciful they bite
>   Thy favourite Bard, O Phoebus, and Physician.
>
> And now I hear a score in union bawl,
>   "In cold contempt shall poor Piozzi sight?
> Miss Hannah More into oblivion fall?
>   Dear Mistress Montague neglected lie?"   (ll. 21–32)

Pindar finds that all of "the mighty cloud-*capp'd* petticoated wise" (l. 42) agree that his verses are measured prose and lack true poetic fire.

It was Hannah More's *Strictures on the Modern System of Female Education* in 1799 which resulted in a dubious honor, a complete satire by Pindar devoted to the lady. The *Monthly Review* (December, 1799, 410–17) found that Miss More's *Strictures* only considered instruction of a moral and religious nature. The reviewer felt that she was too strict in her objection to the restoration of female criminals to society, and he also took her to task for stating that an instructress of youth should have a thorough knowledge of human corruption. Furthermore, Miss More regarded children's parties as unhealthy, objected to any idle pursuits on Sundays, and felt a mother should be taught by a church divine before she attempted to instruct her own children.

Beilby Porteus (1731–1808), Lord Bishop of London, praised Miss More's *Strictures* to his clergy, and the court approved of them; but "royal approval and episcopal eulogy did not prevent a storm of criticism and abuse."[16] Centering his attack on the folly of flattery, Peter Pindar produced *Nil Admirari, or a Smile at a Bishop* (December, 1799). In the prose preface, the satirist states that he is addressing the poem to Dr. Porteus because the bishop compliments "Miss Hannah More on talents that are presumed to have *worked wonders* in the cause of Religion and *high-toned* Morality," and he then adds that no one will ever say the bishop has critical abilities. Pindar next quotes Porteus's own panegyric which sounds more like a satire than a work of praise, for the bishop has found Miss More's instructive work to be "enlivened with such brilliancy of wit, such richness of imagery, such variety and felicity of allusion, such neatness and elegance of diction; as are not, I conceive, easily found combined and blended together in any other work in the English language."

Objecting to this high praise of the "*good* maid" (l. 32), a reference to her spinster status, Pindar the satirist presents his views through metallic metaphors, including mundic (fool's gold):

> Oft by my touchstone have I tried the Lass,
>   And see no shining mark of Gold appear;
> No, nor one beam of silver:—some small *brass*,
>   And *Lead* and glittering *mundic*, in thine ear.   (ll. 33–36)

Wishing to be just, he admits that her life is a very good one; "But then, her verse and Prose are *very bad*" (l. 44). In Part II of the poem he feels that, if Wisdom had stopped her pen and if Silence had gagged her, no mourning crepe would appear on the hill of the Muses. If the bishop had remained silent, waiting Oblivion would have claimed Miss More; but then Porteus is not solely to blame:

> I censure not Miss Hannah for sad Prose;
>   I censure not Miss Hannah for sad Rhymes.
> God sees my heart: I only censure those
>   Whose *flatteries* damn the judgment of the times.

> The *Bas-bleu* Club, grave Greybeards, those old Dames
>   All righteous, cramm'd to mouth with heavenly manna,
> Ambitious of a Wit among their names,
>   Into their *magic lantern* clapp'd Miss Hannah;
>
> Then bade the Bishop *look* with wondering eyes.
>   The Bishop's wondering orbs enjoyed the sight.
> "A Giantess of genius!" Porteus cries,
>   Forgetting it a literary Mite.   (ll. 37–48)

In Part III, the satirist hints that the *Strictures* are not Hannah's own but belong to some parson; and he next questions her piety and benevolence, particularly her views about female criminals:

> Oh, had *good* Hannah been not so severe
>   On each young Victim of her tempting bloom!
> Instead of sarcasm, dropp'd a pitying tear;
>   And with a beam of *comfort* cheer'd her gloom! (ll. 25–28)

Turning to Porteus in Part IV, Peter Pindar informs the bishop that his eulogy may corrupt Miss Hannah by making her prideful:

> Thus then, O Man of God, they flattery *sins*:
>   For thou has conjured up the Woman's vanity;
> Bestowed false consequences on Heads of Pins,
>   And given (oh blush!) a substance to inanity.   (ll. 61–64)

Appending "An Address to Miss Hannah More" to the poem, the poet wonders why she is so critical of poets and suggests the reason may be that no poet has ever praised her; but then things equal themselves out since his verses have been damned by the "blue stockings." Picturing them as dour and aged matrons, he bids the reader view "The toothless gums of half the grave *Bas-bleu/* Watering, and *wondering* how the World can *smile*" (ll. 47–48). Turning directly to these ladies in an "Ode to the Blue-stocking Club," he damns them with honorific adjectives:

> Old Critics, Gammer Wisdoms, *sapient* Dames,
> Who fond of being deem'd *illustrious* names,
>   Proudly o'er Mount Parnassus cast your shoes;
> In grave Divan, who most *sublimely* sit,
> Pronouncing judgment upon Works of Wit,
>   Indeed on all the labours of the Muse;   (ll. 1–6)

Restating his belief that Hannah More may have lifted some or all of her ideas from a priest's notebook, Peter feels that the ladies, for the sake of their own honor and reputations, should make Miss More acknowledge the petty theft. This advice concludes the main attack upon Hannah More except for a prose "Postscript" in which Pindar reviews his own satire for magazines and praises it far more than he censures it.

The last reference to Miss More appears in Canto III of "Orson and Ellen; a Legendary Tale," one of the poems in the miscellany entitled *Tears and Smiles* (December, 1801). In a conversation about various topics between Boniface, an innkeeper, and Orson, a young traveler, a reference is made to Bishop Porteus's critical abilities:

> Thus ended Boniface; and now
>   They talk'd of Hannah More;
> Whose fame the Bishop's trumpets sounds,
>   That makes a mighty roar.
>
> Then on each other did they wink,
>   Which thus might be translated:
> "*Some people* may a mitre wear,
>   And yet be *shallow-pated*." (ll. 53–60)

V *The Satiric Bias*

Wolcot's views of Boswell, Warton, Pye, Bruce, and More are correct only if one side of their characters is examined, However, a satirist, to be effective, often shortens his vision by disregarding a victim's better qualities in order to throw the faults which he alone may observe into high relief. The victim emerges as a caricature of a particular fault or folly since the satirist wishes to teach and to correct, not to present a complex individual's total personality. And Wolcot must be viewed not solely as a literary critic but as a satirist. As a critic, his criticism can be called "impressionistic" since his feelings and his disposition toward a work under examination appear clearly and reflect not only his own views but those of his contemporaries. Content and style are not really at issue, for both are symptomatic of greater error—man's pride in himself or his lack of reason. Boswell and Bruce reflect pride in self; the poet laureates, Porteus, and More reveal lack of reason.

Simply stated, Wolcot, as a satirist, seized upon an event or public personality for renumerative gain. What aroused public interest and what was perhaps glaringly obvious to literary-minded people was written about and commented upon in a manner which offered old ideas and no new rules of criticism. He demands a work to be truthful, reasonable, lively; therefore, the writer must not allow his imagination to control him, he must not self-aggrandize, and he must not be dull. These concepts are not new; they are typical of the satirist's artistic intent of returning an individual to his senses.

What was new—and the reason for which Wolcot was read— was the humorous, mocking slyness with which he attacked prominent individuals. His short, biting metaphors; his half-wondering tone in speaking of faults discovered; his colloquial language; and his ironic advice—all of these qualities gave the reader a vicarious, perhaps malicious, pleasure. He was read, enjoyed, and then dismissed by more recent generations because of his topicality. In his attack on literary figures, he wrote about the concerns of the moment, such as Bruce's *Travels*, as fictitious narrative; and, after the concerns of the moment had passed, the import and impact of his attacks diminished.

CHAPTER 4

The Virtuosi and the Royal Society

SINCE Wolcot found his topics for ridicule in the men of his times
and wrote to make money, he did not always write about artists
or literary figures; rather, he found a subject which would sell a
satire. He often said that the public loved variety, and he gave his
readers different subjects over whom they could assume a sense of
superiority. Thus Wolcot, beginning in 1788, turned his attention
to the Royal Society and its president Sir Joseph Banks. Some
background concerning the Royal Society must be given to understand Wolcot's attitudes and to illustrate that he was probably
writing within a tradition.

The Royal Society, established in 1662 for purposes of scientific
exchanges and endeavors, soon came to have a membership composed chiefly of virtuosi, "amateurs, science-lovers, but not scientists."[1] As Norman Pearson has indicated, the virtuoso in the
seventeenth and eighteenth centuries was regarded as "a contemptible crank, superstitious and gullible, and interested only in
the eccentric or the monstrous: a sham philosopher, vain, and
shallow, whose ostensible love of learning was at root but an idle
curiosity, and whose learning itself was studiously divorced from
practical utility."[2] Thus, many of the experiments and papers by
the members of the Royal Society produced criticism, laughter,
and jokes. Among the early satires against this group, Dorothy
Stinson lists Samuel Butler's "Elephant in the Moon" and his "On
the Royal Society," Thomas Shadwell's play *The Virtuoso*, and
Mrs. Aphra Behn's farce *The Emperor in the Moon*. In the eighteenth century such figures as Addison and Steele, Jonathan Swift,
Edward Young, and also John Hill in his *A Review of the Works
of the Royal Society of London* (1751) satirized the society during
a period when the number of true scientists decreased in proportion
to the increase of historians and antiquarians among its members.[3]
Until 1820, when a reform in membership requirements was undertaken, "the society continued to be mainly an association of science-
lovers, of amateurs, with a growing resemblance to a fashionable
men's club."[4] From this brief introduction to the status of the

Royal Society during John Wolcot's lifetime, the reader may easily perceive that membership in that organization was as honored and as readily ridiculed by the general public as was the post of poet laureate; and the doings of the society were reported in the periodicals of the time and hence familiar to anyone who cared to read about them.

In respect to the Royal Society, it is more convenient to group Wolcot's references to the society's president and to individual members of that body than to examine the scattered commentary chronologically. Briefly stated, the satirist's view of the society's members may be regarded as a traditional one; they are considered as lacking in common sense and reason. Such members examine the particular and the minute, from which no immediate benefit to society (meaning man) can be realized, thus avoiding the general and the practical; furthermore, they illustrate their folly through their journal, the *Transactions of the Royal Society*, which prints accounts of their strange experiments and wild conjectures.

Wolcot's methods are similar to those he developed in his earliest satires: he either states a man is downright foolish or presents him as a wise man and then ridicules the wise one by listing the person's ideas or accomplishments. If the individual under attack defends himself or a friend, he only succeeds in damning through such praise; for it is Peter Pindar who skillfully guides the defense toward the borders of ridiculousness. Highlighting the subject's own pursuits, he offers a scientist some ludicrous project for investigation; he makes both appear full of nonsense. Briefly then, his method is threefold: a piece of pure reportage with emphasis on the ludicrous; advice which suggests inanity or the ridiculous on the subject's part; and, primarily, a friendly, chatty tone as if he were a friend interested in the subject's welfare.

Peter Pindar's critical stance, though not explicitly given, is concerned with a man's being well balanced. If a man, within his own nature or pursuits, leans toward one specialty, such as botany, he may become indifferent to other aspects of living and thus be out of harmony with life. Man, having reason and common sense, could not operate rationally if this distorted view of existence dominated him, as the poem dealing with Sir Joseph Banks's butterfly chase later illustrates. The virtuosi in the Royal Society, be they gentlemen-antiquarians, archeologists, botanists, or inventors, share a propensity toward dabbling in their own specialities which the critic, Peter Pindar, finds sets them apart from general society; and their dabbling and their endeavors are regarded as foolish since these men are not geniuses. Behind all their endeavors, Peter Pindar hints, a portion of vanity and pride may be found. It is plain, however, that the satirist could not see that research, pure or otherwise, might lead to important scientific discoveries, to a broader knowledge of history, or even to an awareness of the functioning of society of the past. Though the satirist was blind in this respect, such blindness makes his stress on immediate practicality more understandable.

To Wolcot, as seen through Peter Pindar, scientific and historic endeavors had to bear a relationship to the present (his generation) and should relate to the general and not to the particular. The world of "little" life—organic life below the level of man—must be avoided; and concentration should be placed on the world of the "great," that which deals with man and attempts to raise him higher. However, the danger involved in dealing with man, as illustrated by the case of Benjamin Thompson, is that a ludicrous particularization may lead astray the seeker after knowledge.

Although this very general rendering of Peter Pindar's views results from his lack of specific advice pertaining to the proper pursuits of scientists and historians, it is clear that his criticism stems from his belief in what constitutes the proper makeup of man. Briefly, then, Peter Pindar, as in most of the satires, wishes to offer an appraisal of folly to enable a self-evaluation to take place which should lead to a readjustment in the way of life of the subject under attack. He appears to say that men are realistic, rationalistic creatures who can, by an examination of their personal quirks, rehabilitate themselves, join general society, and work for its betterment and improvement. Although Wolcot's views were perhaps easily discerned in his satires by his contemporaries, the modern reader needs historical and biographical information to understand them. Wolcot, the reporter, spoke of events known to the readers of periodicals of the times; to recapture the topicality of his remarks, background information must be given.

I   *Presidents*

Sir Joseph Banks (1743–1820), a student of botany, traveled with Captain Cook from 1768 to 1771 on a voyage around the world, became George III's scientific adviser in 1772, and was instrumental in securing Captain Bligh his position as captain of the *Bounty* for the ship's historic cruise to the West Indies. On November 30, 1778, Banks became the president of the Royal Society, a post to which he was annually reelected until his death in 1820; and he probably became the society's president due to a controversy over lightning rods. The American Revolution produced within George III an antipathy toward all things American, including Benjamin Franklin's championing of pointed lightning rods. The king placed blunt-nosed rods on his palace and asked Sir John Pringle, the society's president, "to change its resolution supporting the points," which Pringle refused to do; and his resignation opened the way for the election of Joseph Banks.[6] At the time of Banks's election, 217 of 330 members of the society were nonscientists.[7] Banks increased the efficiency of the society's administration, strengthened the office of president, and tightened admission requirements at the cost of being viewed as either a dictator or a tyrant by some of the members.[8] More in Banks's favor is the fact that under his guidance Kew Gardens, for which people throughout the world sent him plants from various climates, presented a magnificent and varied botanical exhibition.[9] Banks, however, must be finally regarded as "a munificent patron of science rather than an actual worker himself. His own writings are comparatively trifling."[10]

Peter Pindar first mentioned Sir Joseph Banks in Canto II (1787) of *The Lousiad* in lines referring to George III as a man interested only in the minor and minute productions of nature. The king is,

> In short, delighted, with the world of *little*:
> Which West shall paint, and grave Sir Joseph Banks
> Receive from thy historic mouth with thanks;
> Then bid the vermin on the Journals crawl,
> Hop, jump, and flutter, to amuse us all.   (ll. 76–80)

The Royal Society's President Banks is fully dealt with in *Sir Joseph Banks and the Emperor of Morocco, A Tale* (December 1788). The "Proemium" states that though the society's members pity Banks's "pigmy merit" (l. 4), Peter will "try to lift a lame dog o'er a stile" (l. 6). Peter's mock defense declares that, though all the president's learning and three-fourths of his sense could be enclosed in a nutshell, he does have a modest wisdom. When Banks undertakes a task, he is like a Hercules; and, as his experimental dinners illustrate, he "most manfully . . . eats a Bat;/ Eats toads, or tough, or tender, old or young" (ll. 22–23); moreover, his gavel frequently arouses the slumbering members. Banks also has great perseverance as the following story, a search for a rare butterfly called the Emperor of Morocco, reveals.

Banks "Went on a day to catch this game renown'd,/ On vi'lets, dunghills, nettle-tops, and daisies" (ll. 3–4) after he first uttered "The Virtuoso's Prayer" requesting God to grant that he discover something new and strange:

> "Since monsters are my great delight,
> With Monsters charm thy servant's sight,
>   Turn Feathers into Hair:
> Make legs where legs were never seen.
> And Eyes, no bigger than a Pin,
>   And broad as Saucers stare.   (ll. 31–36)

If Banks could discover flies without heads, the members of the Royal Society and the journals would praise him; the headless flies would bear his name. He concludes the prayer, goes butterfly hunting, and sees the rare Emperor of Morocco. No one could be more blessed or happy; and Peter Pindar offers a series of comparisons to illustrate Banks's feelings, one of which is slightly bawdy: "Not with more joy, nor rapture-speaking look,/ The little gamesome Piccadilly Duke/ Eyes a nice *tit*, fresh launch'd upon the Town" (ll. 73–75). Banks pursues the butterfly, strikes with his net, misses; continues the pursuit; often falls, rises, and falls again; but all the while he is intent upon exhibiting the Emperor of Morocco as Tamerlane did the captured Bajazet. So Banks, though nearly out of breath, and covered with mud, continues the pursuit, wildly waving his arms, "Mindless of trees, and bushes, and brambles,/ Head over heels into the lane he scrambles" (ll. 158–59). Over a garden wall flies the game; Sir Joseph follows, knocks down the gardener, and the botany lover is described as a destructive agent obsessed with but one idea:

> O'er peerless hyacinths our Hero rush'd;
> Through tulips and anemonies he push'd,
>   Breaking a hundred *necks* at every spring:
> On bright carnations, blushing on their banks,
> With desperate hoof he trod, and mowed down ranks,
>   Such vast ambition urged to seize the King.   (ll. 175–80)

The scarecrow is knocked down and the beehive is overturned before the butterfly hunter is caught by the gardener, who calls his captive a villain while pointing out the damage done to the garden. Sir Joseph, whose mind is concerned only with his prey, can only declare that the Emperor has flown away. Believing the man to be insane, the gardener curses the keepers for allowing a Bedlamite to escape; and he walks away from the dangerous fellow whom he had captured. The poem concludes with a promise of more sallies upon the president of the Royal Society: "Such is the Tale. If Readers sigh for more,/ Sir Joseph's wallet holdeth many a score" (ll. 267–68).

Peter's Prophecy (December, 1788) is an imaginary conversation between the satirist and Banks in which Banks is told that, at the annual election in November, he will be out of office. Despite Banks's assertion that he will remain in power, Peter indirectly spoofs the man's abilities by advising him to limit his enemies' satisfaction by resigning and retiring to the country:

> Go with your wisdom and amaze the Boors
> With apple-tree, and shrub, and flow'r *amours*;
> And tell them all, with wide-mouth'd wonder big,
> How Gnats can make a Cuckhold of a Fig.
> Form fly-clubs, shell-clubs, weed-clubs if you please,
> And proudly reign the President of *these*.   (ll. 57–62)

Peter hints that Sir Joseph slipped into his place by accident, and he mentions that mathematicians no longer appear in the society's journal. Sir Joseph agrees and, unconsciously damning himself, adds, "Philosophers my soul with horror rend./ Whene'er their mouths are open'd, I am mum:/ Plague take 'em, should a *President* be *dumb*?" (ll. 122–24).

Peter claims that he has often seen Banks trying to grasp at sense just like a spider that claws to retrieve its disturbed thread. When Sir Joseph asks what the world's opinion of him is, Peter replies that it wonders how he can sit on the chair once occupied by Sir Isaac Newton; for "When to the Chair Banks forced his bold ascent,/ He crawl'd a Bug upon the Monument" (ll. 189–90). The world feels Banks is unqualified for his office and that he never wrote a line in the journals. Under him, any trifle hunter who brings "a grub, a weed, a moth, a beetle's wing" (l. 210) can become a member. The Royal Society was once the home of science; but

> Now at the door see moon-eyed Folly grin,
> Inviting Bird's-nest Hunters to come in;
> Idiots who Specks of Eggs devoutly ken,
> And furbish up a Folio on a Wren.
>
> (ll. 225–28)

Sir Joseph says he is famous; he is pointed out wherever he goes. Peter deflates the man's pride by stating that these gawkers are just country people and that true fame comes from the opinion of men of wisdom. The knight's appearances at court do not mean he has worth. Sir Joseph still believes he can beat the opposition in the coming election since he can name, to list his qualifications, the vegetable tribes and also the names of monkeys. Puncturing this wisdom, the satirist, replies, "I grant you, Sir, in Monkey knowledge great;/ Yet say, should Monkeys give you Newton's seat?" (ll. 293–94). The president's labors are more suited to old maids, not to men of great minds; and, though he may know many anecdotes, such knowledge is not enough, for any gossip could claim the chair.

After a series of remarks by Peter on various members of the society and on the love of antiquarians for old cracked pottery, Sir Joseph exclaims, "Poh, pox! don't laugh;—such things are rich and scarce;/ Be *something* sacred; let not *all* be farce" (ll. 485–86). After the satirist claims that he must laugh when such things as these please the many, he returns to his main point and tells Sir Joseph that experimental dinners no longer please the society members; they want something more than Banks can produce. Mistaking the point of the remark, Banks, after repeating the list of delicacies eaten, exclaims, "And must the villains still have *something new?*/ Tell then each petty President-creator, God damn him, that I'll eat an *alligator!*" (ll. 614–16). Banks should not eat an alligator, concludes the poem; instead, he should

> Feast on the Arts and Sciences, and learn
> Sublimity from Trifle to discern:
> With shells, and flies, and daisies, covered o'er,
> Let Pert Queen Fiddlefaddle rule no more.
>
> Thus shall Philosophy her suffrage yield,
> Sir Joseph wear his Hat, and Hammer wield;
> No more shall Wisdom on the Journals *stare*,
> Nor Newton's image *blush* behind the Chair.   (ll. 617–26)

Subjects for Painters contains two thrusts at the president of the society. One, in the very beginning, illustrates Banks's misplaced knowledge and scientific curiosity, for he proved "his superior *classic* taste,/ By swallowing the sumen of a Pig" (ll. 293–94). (An explanation of this delicacy appears in this chapter in the section dealing with Sir William Hamilton.) The other reference, entitled "Sir Joseph Banks and the Thief-takers", relates a true incident in the man's life and manages to use "simpling" as an adjective in respect to Banks and also as a verb:

> Sir Joseph, favorit of *great* Queens and Kings;
> Whose wisdom, Weed and Insect Hunter sings;
>   And Ladies fair applaud, with smile so dimpling;
> Went forth one day, admidst the laughing fields,
> Where Nature such exhaustless treasure yields,
>   A simpling!   (ll. 1–6)

While searching for plants in a ditch, Banks, against his protests, is seized by bailiffs who search his pockets only to discover frogs, toads, flowers, and weeds. Claiming that Banks's face reveals him to be a thief, they drag him to the squire who recognizes Sir Joseph and reprimands the zealous bailiffs. The officers vow that they will no longer judge others hereafter by their appearances.

Recapitulating the subjects of his previous satires in the opening lines of *A Benevolent Epistle to Sylvanus Urban*, Peter implies that a lack of reason and common sense is the lot of Sir Joseph Banks,

> Who, scorning Suns and Moons, with *happier* eyes,
> Beholds from dunghills purple Emperors rise!
> More blest on *this* our earth a Frog to see,
> To find a Cockleshell, and boil a Flea,
> Then dwell in yonder Skies, with glory Crown'd
> Where Frogs, nor Fleas, nor Cockle-shells, abound;
> More blest to mark a Bat's than Angel's wing,
> To hear a Grasshopper than Seraph sing;
> More pleased to view (if Rumor justly paints)
> The *tails* of tadpoles than the *heads* of Saints,
> And hear (to Fame if credence may be giv'n)
> One Humming-bird than all the Host of Heaven:— (ll. 13–17)

The conclusion to this satire about the publisher of the *Gentlemen's Magazine* contains a short anecdote, "Sir Joseph and the Boiled Fleas." One morning while his employer is at breakfast with a number of Royal Society members, Jonas Dryander (1748–1810), Banks's librarian, enters to tell Sir Joseph that he has boiled fifteen hundred fleas but not one changed color. This news causes Banks to grumble under his breath until the members present demand to know what is wrong. Striding around the room and angry with disappointment, Sir Joseph says, "'Since you *must* know, *must* know' (he sighed) "'the meaning,—/ Fleas are *not* lobsters, damn their souls'" (ll. 83–84). The "Argument" to the poem claims that Dryander had collected the fifteen hundred fleas from Sir Joseph's bed.

A reply to this attack on Sir Joseph Banks is found in *A Rowland for an Oliver* (June, 1790) supposedly written by John Nichols, who wonders how the satirist can attack the universally admired Sir Joseph. Since Wolcot guides the pen, Nichols supports the satirist's views even though he is defending the scientist. Nichols, in trying to reveal Banks's admirable reputation, says, according to Pindar:

> Even from the North and South, and West and East,
> Men send him Shell, and Butterfly, and Beast.
> Sir William Hamilton sends Gods and Mugs;
> And, for his feast, a Sow's most dainty Dugs.
> And shall such Mob as thou, not worth a groat,
> Dare pick a hole in *such* a great man's coat? (ll. 161–66)

Canto III (April, 1791) of *The Lousiad* lists the various portraits to be found in the mansion of the Goddess of Discord, and "There curs'd Sir Joseph Banks, in quest of fame,/ At finding Fleas and Lobsters not the same" (ll. 181–82). Canto IV (December, 1792) offers a series of comparisons dealing with the strange dichotomy existing between the nature of the private and the public man.

> Sir Joseph, Jove-like, with his Hammer'd Arm,
> Who thundering breaks of sleep the opiate charm;
> And *that* Sir Joseph, with a simple look,
> Collecting simples near the simple brook. (ll. 230–34)

Canto V (December, 1795) speaks of how ambition makes the wise seem like fools. Why ambition,

> Bade round the World the famed Sir Joseph float
> To kiss Queen Oberea in the boat;
> And spurs him now his blood's last drop to shed,
> In quest of Butterflies without a Head. (ll. 316–19)

The reference to Queen Oberea can be traced to *An Account of the Voyages Undertaken by the Order of His Present Majesty for Making Discoveries in the Southern Hemisphere* by John Hawkesworth, published in 1773, which dealt with Cook's voyage on which Banks was a member. Oberea was not "Queen of Tahitie," yet she managed to convince members of the expedition that she was, and Banks's meeting with her was mentioned. The Oberea-Banks meeting led to two anonymous satires, *An Epistle from Oberea, Queen of Otaheite, to Joseph Banks, Esq.* (1773) and *An Epistle from Mr. Banks, Voyager, Monster-hunter, and Amoroso, to Oberea, Queen of Othaheite* (1774), which made fun of Banks's discomforts on Tahiti and presented him and Oberea as lovers.

Pindariana: or Peter's Portfolio (1794), a collection of serious and satirical poems on various subjects, has four references to Banks. The following poem, "Early Propensities," is given in its entirety:

> How early, genius shows itself at times!
> Thus Pope, the pride of Poets, *lisp'd* in Rhymes;
>   And *thus* the great Sir Joseph (strange to utter!)
> To whom each insect-eater is a fool
> Did, when a little boy at school,
>   Munch *spiders* spread upon his bread and butter.

The "Ode to Coffee," concerning the poet's reflections while drinking that beverage, refers to the Royal Society president as the poet does "at his rare merit wonder,/ In flies and tadpoles deep" (ll. 26–27). The poem immediately following, entitled simply "Ode", deals with man's susceptibility to flattery:

> Show me the man, and I will thank thee for it,
> Who says, with truth, "Poh! Flattery? I abhor it."—
> 'Tis a *non-descript* by Sir Joseph bred;
> A Soho *monster*, born without a head.   (ll. 13–16)

The last reference in this collection is found in "Ode to the Butter-fly" in which the poet states he would protect this creature from Sir Joseph's net and from the nets of others who are wild to make collections. If the butterfly were captured, it would be shown to a rapturous Banks and his friends; it would be mentioned fully in the society's journal, "And even thy pretty mealy painted wing/ Employ description sweet, for fifty pages" (ll. 17–18).

A brief reference (ll. 175–80) is made by Pindar to Sir Joseph in *The Royal Tour* (1795) when he is presented as a collector of butter-flies, grubs, nests, hummingbird's eggs, newts, tadpoles, beetle brains, and stings of bees. In *One Thousand Seven Hundred and Ninety-Six* (1797), Peter speaks of individuals falsely praised and says,

> Tell Banks he fills with *honour* Newton's Chair,
> The weed-and-bird's-nest-hunter will not *stare*:
> Aloud with Newton's fancied powers he brays,
> And struts with Newton down to distant days.   (1, 243–46)

The last major reference to Sir Joseph occurred when he was made a member of the privy council on March 13, 1797.[11] "On a Report in the Newspaper that Sir Joseph Banks was made a Privy Counseller" appeared in Pindar's *An Ode to the Livery of London* (July, 1797). Claiming that this appointment is some kind of hoax passed off on the public which believes anything Pitt says, Peter states Banks is no political expert, only an excellent catcher of butterflies, and "an intellectual Flea" (l. 39) who parasitically feeds off science. If the report were true, there would certainly be a clash of personalities and temperaments, for, while Pitt would be talking about France, Spain, or loans, Sir Joseph would be thinking about beetles, flies, toads, tadpoles, weeds, and snails. If Pitt were thinking about army supplies, Sir Joseph would be thinking about Flea or louse traps, "or, deep-studying makes/ A Pair of Breeches for a Frog" (ll. 73–74). If a moth appeared during a debate, Banks, using his hat for a net, would chase it and create a riot. The king should heed the story of the cat who asked Jupiter to transform her into a lady, which the god did. One night in bed, she heard a rat, caught it like a cat, and for this the god changed her back into an animal. Since it is difficult to change one's nature, George III should make Banks a grub hunter again.

In a footnote to this satire, Peter Pindar reports that the knight has truly become a privy consellor, and now Ridicule enjoys a second laugh; the first laugh was uttered when the man became president of the Royal Society. While defending satiric thrusts at Banks, Pindar kindly offers some advice: "Sir Joseph must not complain at his being so frequently the subject of a poetical laugh: Folly is the natural and fair *game* of Satire. To wreck his revenge on the Muse, by condemning her to silence, let him cease to play the fool."

II   *Of Scientists and Antiquarians*

Minor references are made to other members of the Royal Society in Peter Pindar's works. Sir Joseph Banks was singled out only because he was the prime representative, due to his position as president, of the lack of sense and reason found in most of the society's members. To understand the satirist's attempts to bring man back to sanity through the exposure of man's folly—an awkward appeal to reason when it is not supposed to exist in the subject under attack—background information must be given to illustrate what Wolcot regards as the nadir of intellect in scientists of the times. Part of Wolcot's success with his publications lies, as the quotations will reveal, with his name-calling of the great while using imagery—dumplings, cockroach, rags—known by and easily visualized by the meanest intellect.

One of Sir Joseph Banks's friends was Sir William Hamilton (1730–1803), the British envoy to Naples from 1764 to 1800, the archeologist who wrote a number of papers for the Royal Society on volcanic erruptions in Italy, and the collector of antiquities which he excavated near Naples. In 1767, Hamilton presented a collection of volcanic earth and materials to the British Museum; and, from 1772 to 1784, he presented or sold the museum a vast collection of Greek and Roman antiquities, including vases, glass, bronzes, gems, coins, and other miscellaneous pieces.[12] In *Peter's Prophecy* (1788), Sir Joseph said that Sir William has supported him for president and had sent him the present of the sumen of a pig, and Peter cast some doubt on the man's sensibilities. In a footnote to identify Sir William and his gift, the satirist wrote, "Sir William Hamilton, who sent Sir Joseph from Italy this *precious* present. The mode of making it properly is, by tying the teats of a Sow, soon after she hath littered, continuing the ligature till the poor creature is nearly exhausted with torture, and then cutting her throat. The effects of the Milk diffused through the Belly-part are so *delicious*, as to be thought to make *ample atonement* for the barbarity." As for Sir William as a scientist and an antiquarian, the poem casts some doubt on Hamilton's integrity and honesty. To the top of Mount Vesuvius he may have "March'd up and clapp'd his nose into the crater,/ Just with the same *sang froid* that Joan the Cook/ Casts on her Dumplings in the Pot a look" (ll. 228–330), but as to his archeological discoveries, the world says "That half Sir William's Mugs and Gods are *new;/ Himself* the *baker* of th'Etrurian ware" (ll. 332–33); it is also rumored that he will soon return to Naples "To bake new Mugs and Gods some ages older" (l. 338).

"A Lyric Epistle to Sir William Hamilton" found in *Odes to Kien Long, the Present Emperor of China* (November, 1792), was occasioned by, according to the satirist, the recent discovery of Gabis, a town buried during the Vesuvius eruption which destroyed Herculaneum, Pompei, and Paestum. Sir. William will have the pleasure of unearthing "*More* broken pans, *more* Gods, *more* mugs,/ *More* snivel-bottles, jordans, and old jugs,/ *More* saucepans, lamps, and candlesticks, and kettles" (ll. 3–5). The antiquarian-archeologist is advised to search throughout the town and send back "God's legs, and legs of old joint-stools,/ Would ravish all our Antiquarian schools" (ll. 19–20). If any gold is discovered, inscribed or not, he is to send it to the king and queen who like plain gold just as well as coined gold.

A prose footnote describes the methods of this antiquarian: "Sir Williams keeps an old antiquarian to *hunt* for him, who when he stumbles on a tolerable statue, *bathes* him in *urine, buries* him, and, when *ripe* for *digging up*, they proclaim a *great discovery* to be made, and out comes an antique for universal admiration!" He also refers to Hamilton's recent marriage, hinting that the bride is no virgin and that Hamilton had better lock the door lest she ramble or go astray to Hedge Lane, "the resort of the Cyprian corps." The bride, Emma Lyon, became the Lady Hamilton romantically linked with Admiral, Lord Nelson. Wolcot implies that Hamilton either cannot recognize the genuine article or he is the victim of shrewd people.

Richard Gough (1735–1809), an antiquarian and a contributor to the *Gentleman's Magazine*, was usually mocked because of his association with publisher John Nichols; but "Elegy to Mr. Richard Gough" in *Tristia* (1806) is devoted to the man's antiquarian pursuits in respect to the arrival of Nile artifacts. Again, Peter Pindar presents the view that such scientific pursuits and specialty results in a deviation from sense, reason, and decorum. Gough peers "Now o'er a Mummy's precious leg or loin/ Devoutly tasting and devoutly smelling,/ Now licking an old Dish, and now a Coin" (ll. 3–4); the results of such research is the "trumpery that every month regales/ The readers of the *Gemman's* Magazine" (ll. 7–8). Gough should come to London and identify the Nile artifacts, thus making the virtuosi giddy with rapture. Discoveries are waiting for the man, and Peter Pindar imagines the river Nile searching its waters for tons of material:

> I see, I see, arrive from Egypt's lands,
>   Gods of old times, and Godlings, green and blue;
> Ribs of its ancient kings, and legs and hands;
>   To ravish all the lovers of *virtù*.   (ll. 29–32)

Since a rag of Joseph's coat and Lady Potiphar's fingers may be exhibited, Gough should hurry to town and wake up the guards lest the valuables be stolen.

One of the earliest references to a virtuoso appears in *Lyric Odes to the Royal Academicians for 1785.* "Ode XXI" refers to Daines Barrington (1727–1800) who read many papers before the Royal Society and the Society of Antiquaries. For the latter he wrote a paper on "Dolly Pentreath, the old woman with whom the Cornish Language expired."[13] "Ode XXI" called "To Myself" begins with a general question as to the poet's birthplace; posterity will eagerly want to know if Peter Pindar was born in Mevagizzy or Mousehold, both in Cornwall. Though he never answers the question, Peter in the reference to Mousehold presents Barrington as a slighty mad antiquarian:

> Hail, *Mousehold*! birth-place of old Doll Pentreath,
>   To *last* who jabber'd Cornish, so says Daines,
> Who, bat-like, haunted ruins, land, and heath,
>   With Will-o-wisp, to brighten up his brains:—
>
> Daines! who a thousand miles, unwearied, trots,
>   For bones, brass farthings, ashes, and old pots;
> To prove that folks of old, like *us*, were made
>   With heads, eyes, hands, and toes, to drive a trade (ll. 21–28)

In *Peter's Prophecy* (1788), when Sir Joseph Banks asks Peter what he thinks of Daines Barrington, the satirist frankly states that Daines lacks sense: "*Think*, of a man denied by Nature *brains*!/ Whose trash so oft the Royal Leaves disgraces;/ Who knows not Jordans brown, from Roman vases!" (ll. 450–52).

Wolcot's views of the senseless pursuits of some scientists in general is briefly seen in *Instructions to a Celebrated Laureat* (1787).

In it, George III is described as peeking into nooks and crannies of Whitbread's brewery, asking inane questions, and this is compared to the minute knowledge gained by the studies of the virtuosi:

> Thus, to the world of *great* whilst others crawl,
> Our Sovereign peeps into the world of *small*:
> Thus microscopic Geniuses explore
>   Things that too oft provoke the public scorn;
> Yet swell of useful knowledge the store,
>   By finding Systems in a Pepper-corn. (ll. 225–30)

The satirist's view of what antiquarians regard as valuable is equally severe in *Peter's Prophecy*:

> Rare are the Buttons of a Roman's Breeches,
> In Antiquarian eyes surpassing Riches:
> Rarr is each crack'd, black, rotten, earthen Dish,
> That held of ancient Rome the flesh and fish:
> Rare are the Talismans that drove the Devil,
> And rare the Bottles that contain'd old Snivel. (ll. 473–78)

In the same satire, Peter Pindar minimizes the scientific observations of John Hunter who is satirically treated by a piece of reportage in a footnote: "John Hunter actually received the Society's gold medal for three papers: viz. on Sow-gelding; on the Wolf, Jackal, and Dog; *proving incontestably*, what the world *knew before*, that the aforesaid animals were *bona fide* of the same species; also on the Loves of Whales." Also in the same work, Charles Blagdon, the Royal Society secretary, is revealed as a scientist who conducts bizarre and useless experiments. In the following lines, Wolcot has in mind Blagdon's paper "Experiments and Observations in a Heated Room," published in the society's journal for 1775:[14]

> Lo! to improve of man the soaring mind,
> For sacred Science, to his skin unkind,
> Did Doctor Blagden in an oven bake,
> Brown as burnt Coffee or a Barley-cake. (ll. 409–412)

III   *American Benjamin Thompson*

Wolcot's last satire on a member of the Royal Society deserves special attention since he devoted an entire pamphlet to the subject and did not add extraneous material to increase its bulk. Although fascinating in itself, it is not necessary to trace the career of Sir Benjamin Thompson, Count von Rumford (1753–1814), in his rise from the village of North Woburn, Massachusetts, to his knighting in 1783 for services to Britain during the American Revolution, to his receiving the title in 1791 of Count of the Holy Roman Empire, and, finally, to his last years after his marriage to the widow of Lavoisier.[15] More important are his *Essays, Political, Economical and Philosophical* (in four volumes, appearing from 1796 to 1801) and his 1799 proposal for the founding of the Royal Institution of Great Britain which was established March 11, 1800, for the purpose of diffusing new scientific information and of teaching the useful application of science, an interest stemming form Thompson's work on food, stoves, and cooking utensils.[16]

The *Monthly Review* for June, 1799 (238), printed a fine compliment to Thompson while reviewing his *Proposals for Forming by Subscription, in the Metropolis of the British Empire, a Public Institution for diffusing the Knowledge and facilitating the general Introduction of useful Mechanical Inventions and Improvements, and for teaching, by Courses of Philosophical Lectures and Experiments, the Application of Science to the common Purposes of Life* (1799). The anonymous reviewer stated: "With unceasing activity, he has exerted himself to increase the convenience of life, and to enlarge the stock of human happiness. In founding the present institution, he seems desirous of perpetuating his benevolence, and of ensuring a continuance of that activity which labours to attain what Bacon calls the true and legitimate goal of Science; the endowment of life with new inventions, and new sources of abundance. May success continue to crown his laudable endeavors!" (238).

Only a few general comments need be made about Thompson's accomplishments: "The cooking of food, and the warming of houses economically, occupied his thoughts, as well as smoky chimneys, five hundred of which he claimed to have cured."[17] In Munich, he engaged in the study of "foodstuffs, light, and heat, and chimney fireplaces"; but "his major achievement in the scientific world (was), namely, the recognition of heat as a mode of molecular motion."[18] Thompson's essays, however, are filled with "dry detail"; and in them "the meat of his accomplishment lies buried under the thick unpalatable gravy of his verbiage, and when, with eyes uplifted, he pauses to philosophize, his lofty sentiments,

somehow, fail to convince."[19] James Alden Thompson finds that
Count Rumford "was an organizer of marked ability and an
excellent showman. But he was unbelievably coldblooded, inordi-
nately egotistic, inherently a snob."[20] W. J. Sparrow considers
him a self-centered man who "was driven always to establish some
form of ascendancy either of rank, power, experience or intellect."[21]
Keeping in mind Count Rumford's improvements on kitchen
utensils such as roasters, his views on smoky chimneys, the publication of his *Essays*, and the establishment of the Royal Institution,
the satire by John Wolcot on this friend of the Royal Society is
easily understandable.

A Poetical Epistle to Benjamin Count Rumford (August, 1801)
begins with a listing of the satirist's previous subjects, and then the
author says he must now speak of a man who came "To build on
smoke his fortune and his fame" (l. 12). All kitchen utensils such
as knives, forks, platters, and the like, should rejoice at the name
of this "Knight of the Dishclout" (l. 29); and every parlor "Boasts
of thy stoves, and talks of nought but thee" (l. 34). One cannot escape mentioning the count's name since every periodical reports his
views, which are honorifically referred to by the satirist:

> Through Newspaper, through Magazine, Review,
> Happy mine eyes thy splendid track pursue;
> Thy sage Opinion in each Journal read,
> A vein of Silver 'midst a load of Lead.   (ll. 39–42)

The Count will rise higher than all the members of the Royal
Society, and the satirist ironically applauds Rumford's studies on
foodstuffs which resulted in wonderous discoveries:

> Great Man, whose power inventive daily rakes
> Balm from a bog, and dinners from a jakes!
> Great man, whose fertile genius could contrive
> To soften rocks, and *flay* the flints *alive*;
> And make (though Envy unbelieving grins)
> Pouches and handsome purses from their *skins*;   (ll. 75–80)

Rumford even teaches the populace the proper method of chewing
food, invents new dishes for them, and may even find a way, a hint
to the inventor, of turning fiddlestrings into vermicelli or of turning
sheep dung into a plum pudding: "And, with Sir Joseph's leave,
with Fish might pass/ His Fleas, his *favourite* Fleas, for Lobster-

sauce" (ll. 125–126). The poet feels it is insolent to give advice to
such an inventive man; however, since Rumford will have a conversation room at the Royal Institution, Pindar suggests that he
"Extend the thought by Love delicious led:/ And give of Graham
the *celestial Bed.*/ *In*, would Subscriptions like a Torrent pour"
(ll. 177–79). The reference to James Graham, the quack doctor
in business from 1779 to 1782 who exhibited, in his Temple of
Health, a "celestial bed" which promised relief from sterility,[22]
may illustrate the beginning of Peter Pindar's declining popularity
since such a reference would be obscure to younger readers in 1802.

The satirist continues to list ridiculous inventions which Rumford
might produce for the public benefit: a roast which turns itself on
the spit, dumplings which boil without a pot, pins to pursue fleas,
handkerchiefs which wipe the nose, and church desks which pour
out prayers. Only envy, Peter ironically claims, makes the wits
call the man an impostor, a hack of folly, or the emperor of quacks—
a device which allows the satirist to level the charge while denying
it. Even Sir Joseph Banks is jealous, and he racks his burned-out
brain, attempting to eclipse the count by planning more experimental
dinners. In desperation, Banks even ordered Dryander to reboil
his fleas; but Rumford need not worry: "*Great Scholarship* with
wisdom link'd is *rare*/ Yet these unite in thee I do declare" (ll. 269–
70). It is clear that Peter Pindar means exactly the opposite of the
above statement; and, in his parting shot, he explicitly reveals how
low in esteem he places the inventor. Since books are sent to Rumford to win his smile, Peter asks him to accept a book containing a
life similar to the count's, the history of "The *laughable*, the *immortal*
Mister Punch" (l. 282).

In treating Rumford, Wolcot has followed stylistic techniques
which he used with other figures of the times: the mock encomium,
the pseudo-advice, the denial of charges against the man while
listing the charges, and sly comparison of the man to a low figure
which sets him in proper perspective. His indirect advice, more
direct in other satires, is that man should use his reason and common
sense and should join the rest of humanity by foregoing folly and
eccentricity. Only after the specialists cease their bizarre studies
will Peter Pindar cease his attacks. Since the world, however, is
filled with many human examples of folly in action, Peter Pindar
found other professions to present before the public for purgative
laughter.

CHAPTER 5

Reviewers, Publishers, and Booksellers

A LTHOUGH John Wolcot did handsomely by his publications, he frequently expressed his antipathy toward reviewers, publishers, and booksellers. Reviewers were regarded as individuals seeking to express their own wit at the expense of an author's labors; booksellers were viewed as exploiters of authors; and publishers, namely those individuals connected with the *Gentleman's Magazine* and the *British Critic,* were presented as negators of works of value and as boosters of books appealing to specialized interests. Once again Wolcot scattered his comments throughout various satires which means that a unified view of his opinions can only be established by disregarding chronology and by grouping his comments on reviewers, publishers, and booksellers in order to consider each group separately.

Wolcot's views and opinions need not be defended, for they follow a pattern with which all satire deals. The members of these satirized groups, consciously or unconsciously, are responsible for productions which lack substance, and their minds exhibit a weakness for what is of little value. They, like parasites, subsist on the talents of writers, but they themselves are not creative; since each regards his profession as a trade, all are businessmen who are interested in sales, not quality. The publishers and the reviewers are most castigated since both can affect the livelihood of an author: the former, by judging a work by its quantity or lack thereof; the latter, by a desire to be witty at an author's expense or by writing from ill-will and malice, not from disinterestedness.

Peter Pinder attacks these groups by using different methods. Pretending he has never called them names, he lists the names he never used. At other times, he calls them vipers, carrion crows, or beasts to illustrate their nature. Seeking to solicit sympathy by declaring he is without friends, Peter writes a review of his own work, and it becomes a parody of the type of book reviews written in the eighteenth century. In respect to John Nichols and his friends, he criticizes the contents of the *Gentleman's Magazine* and the works of its publisher. Allowing John Nichols to defend himself, Peter presents a man who unconsciously reveals himself to be a fool. Pindar implies that the staff of the *British Critic* are hypocrites since they lack impartiality, a quality which a critic should possess. Humorously referring to himself as mild mannered, he claims they cannot recognize his genius, which posterity will discover.

One device frequently used is the honorific reference. The term "gentlemen" in italics is applied to Pindar's enemies; and the constant repetition of it, as well as his other statements, reveals that it is an empty title. The mock-honorific adjective and the mock encomium are his frequent methods to deflate or to attack a personality. Critical reportage, such as commentary on a person's works, is also frequently used and in a vein similar to that of book reviews of the period. All in all, the devices which Wolcot employs are certainly not new, nor is the pervading irony found in his critiques. What is refreshing, however, is the tone of most of his critiques. Though he frequently speaks to a specific person, a third party, the reader, is always present; and this third party sees the shy, sly smile of the satirist or the wink of his eye. Writing on what might affect him personally, however, produces a change; the thought of writers' precariously dependent relationship with publishers produces vituperative language and a feeling which is an amalgam of rage and despair. Perhaps this change in style merely means that folly and stupidity which strike close to home cannot be treated urbanely because personal involvement colors opinion. It does seem true that Peter Pindar is at his best and happiest when he satirizes such individuals as James Boswell, James Bruce, and Count Rumford with whom he had no personal contact.

I Reviewers

In *A Poetical, Supplicating, Modest, and Affecting Epistle to Those Literary Colossuses, The Reviewers* (August, 1778), published anonymously, Pindar damns the reviewers through a form of ocupatio by listing the insults which the poet claims he never uttered. Wolcot begins by stating his modest aspirations and his hope that the reviewer will be kind to his future publications since he likes to eat well. He claims that he should receive kind treatment because he never said that they murdered authors "With hatchets, scalping-knives, in shape of pens" (1. 19); nor did he say that in their reviews "The limbs of butcher'd Writers, cheek by jowl/

Look'd like the legs of Flies on cobwebs hung/ Before the hungry Spider's dreary hole" (ll. 22–24). No, never has he said anything against these "men of classic fame" (1. 30) "Whose *dictum* saves at once or damns a name" (1. 32). He never said they fed on authors "Like carrion Crows upon a poor dead Horse" (1.36) or that they sold their praise for a half-crown. And the "No, for I know you'd spurn the *paltry* bribe" (1. 44) skillfully suggests that they can be bribed but only by larger sums.

Claiming others have called reviewers boldly proud, Pindar has regarded them as true oracles and has often defended them. It is quite all right if they praise their own writings: "Zounds! is not justice due to one's dear *self?*/And should not charity begin at *home?*" (ll. 71–2). They make no hasty judgments upon a book; "But first at ev'ry Coffee-house inquire,/How in their favour runs the public tide" (ll. 117–18). Everyone fears their impartial criticism since even Samuel Johnson and Charles Churchill were "Crack'd with that ease a beggar cracks his lice" (1. 134). Since reviewers are so powerful, the poet hopes his petition for kind treatment will be granted, and he allows the reviewers to quote as much from his works as they please.

The nature of Wolcot as a topical satirist is evident here in his early work, and it indicates that an annotated or footnoted edition of Wolcot's works is needed to see Wolcot as a gossipy reporter of his times. To the reviewers, he says he will allow them to extract as much as they please from his works—"I'll put no angry face on;/Nor fill a hungry Lawyer's fist with fees,/To trounce a Bookseller, like furious Mason" (ll. 140–42), a reference to the lawsuit William Mason (1724–1797) had successfully brought against the publisher John Murray in 1777 for printing extracts from Mason's biography of Thomas Gray.

The *Epistle to the Reviewers* closes with "An Address to the Reviewers" in which the poet states his true feelings. It is a pity no higher court of appeal exists, and he wishes to remain uncriticized by these false critics who are but "usurpers of the critic throne" (1. 19). The damaging effects of a critic's low opinion of an author's work is used in Canto III (1791) of *The Lousiad* to describe the faces of the cooks who know their heads must be shaved:

> Not with less pleasure doth a Poet look
> On cruel Criticism, which damns his Book,

Or recommends it to that peaceful shore
Where Books and Bards are never heard of more:—
Then look'd each man, with lengthen'd boding beard,
On that sad morn, which doom'd them to be shear'd.

"Ode IX" of the *Expostulatory Odes* (1789) finds that the man who commits his poetry to the public often has placed it in a lion's mouth, for the world laughs at his pains. Hungry individuals attack it because abuse sells well; even the lamblike Peter has been attacked. He ironically asks, "Why am I persecuted for my Rhymes,/That *kindly* try to cobble Kings and Times?" (ll. 33–34). He seemed to become more sensitive to criticism, for he added an "Address to my Book, an Elegy" to *The Remonstrance* (1791); and in it he warned his pamphlet that its virtues would be hidden and that it would be called a thing made of lead. Spite and hunger, he writes, produced these attacks since reviewers are not men but merely apprentice boys, louts, or riddle makers; these men are merely eunuchs in the land of taste who wish to set fire to everything which has been written.

In a prose "Postscript" to *Nil Admirari* (1799), Peter Pindar writes that—since he has no friends among the reviewers and fears foul treatment of his latest work "which, in a moment of spleen or ignorance, may be put to death by the tomahawk of Criticism" —he will give a free and impartial account of his pamphlets by imitating "a Reviewer totally unconnected with the Author." This leads to a humorous review for those familiar with eighteenth-century journals since his review follows the general pattern of general statement, praise, criticism, and general summary statement found in the book-review sections. Peter begins his "impartial" account by stating that works of genius are rare and that the opportunity to offer honest praise is now embraced. Peter, claims the review, has improved but still retains the same fire, originality, irony, and luxuriancy of imagination; "Such a combination of various and opposite talents we never witnessed in the same writer." Each piece and point is praised, and the reviewer feels compelled to censure those other reviewers who attempt to obscure this writer's talents. The conclusion, a diatribe upon the critics, is one of the most damning statements written by Peter Pindar: "Instead of coming forwards as the fair and candid interpreters of the Muses, they are too many of them the partial trumpeters of their own pigmy pretensions; or despicable pimps, hired to debauch the public taste, and mislead the judgment; to displace the statue of Genius, to make room for those of Arrogance and Folly."

The miscellaneous collection of odds and ends in verse and prose entitled *Pindariana: or Peter's Portfolio* (1794) offers sound advice to authors in respect to reviewers' opinions. In "Prologue. To The Critics," Pindar advises, "Brother-Authors, attend unto the wisdom of Peter. Are the cries of the malevolent and envious against you; be silent, and let your Works fight their own battle. Are they good for nothing; let them die. Possess they merit; they need not be afraid; bid your Minds then sit calmly on their thrones, amidst the hurly-burly of *critical* attacks." This advice may be sound, but Wolcot's haste in composition may account for but not excuse the awkward image in which the mind sits on its throne.

The last general statement on reviewers appears in *Tristia* (1806) in "Elegy"[1] which pictures them as deadly vipers who can be rendered nonlethal through the offering of a coin or a meal, but poor Peter is too impoverished to pay for praise with a dinner or porter. These men can ruin an author, and it is only their power which makes them welcome to a home, for *"Who* dares *affront* such formidable writers;/Snakes, whose sharp fangs inflict a wound?"* (ll. 7–8).

II John Nichols and the Gentleman's Magazine

John Nichols (1745–1826), printer and author, was apprenticed in 1757 to William Bowyer (1699–1777), the publisher of the *Gentleman's Magazine* "by Sylvanus Urban."[2] Nichols, with David Henry, managed this magazine from 1778 to 1792 and from 1792 was solely responsible for it until his death.[3] Nichols's literary productions will be mentioned later, but it should now be stated that, as a Fellow of the London Society of Antiquaries, Nichols published material, such as discussions on ancient coins, which would interest such a group, in his magazine. Under Nichols, the *Gentleman's Magazine* earned a trustworthy reputation, especially in the fields of topography, antiquities, and biography.[4] The specialized interests of Nichols revealed by his own writings, the contents of his magazine, and the reviews of Peter Pindar's satires therein produced many attacks on the man from John Wolcot. These attacks can be viewed as stemming partially from a response to inane material which illustrates a vacuity of mind on the part of Nichols. A chronological arrangement of these attacks shows that a review or an event played a part in their publication.

"Ode XIII" of the *Expostulatory Odes* (1789) finds the poet complaining that everyone attacks him, for "Lo, every puppy *lifts his leg* at Peter" (1. 8). It seems to be a critical tempest; "Indeed it must be dread,/When from his shop John Nichols pops his head,/ And pours the thunders of his Magazine" (ll. 15–17). However, Pindar must take the man seriously, even though the world laughs and regards Nichols as another Hudibras, that hypocritical protestant knight in Samuel Butler's poem of the same name.

In *Subjects for Painters* (1799), Peter Pindar has Benjamin West criticize his verse; and, in the process, he attacks John Nichols for his *Biographical and Literary Anecdotes of William Bowyer* (1782) and for his *Miscellaneous Tracts by the late William Bowyer and several of his Friends* (1786). Nichols's friend Richard Gough (1735–1809), an antiquarian who contributed to the *Gentleman's Magazine* and who was interested in coins and medals, is also ridiculed. West, wishing to belittle Peter Pindar's poems, invidiously compares him with Nichols:

> "Thy very Bellman's Rhymes possess more merit:
> Nay, Nichols' Magazine exceeds in spirit;
> A printer's Devil, with conceit so drunk,
> Who publishes for *gentleman* and *trunk*;
>
> "Who sets up Author on old Bowyer's scraps;—
> Bowyer, whose pen recorded all the raps
> That hungry Authors gave to Bowyer's door,
> To swell the *curious* literary store:
>
> "Who on a purblind Antiquarian's back,
> A founder'd, broken-winded hack,
>   Rides out to find old farthings, nails, and bones;
> On *darkest* coins the *brightest* Legend reads,
> On *traceless* copper *sees* imperial heads,
>   And makes Inscriptions *older* than the stones   (ll. 161–74)

Missing from the 1812 edition of Wolcot's works, but included in the 1794 edition, is the following note: "Mister West is not a judge. John's *Magazine* is a sad *farrago*, possessing, however, the merit of being more in *quantity* than other magazines; as for the *quality*, John who is a most *excellent tradesman*, deemeth it of no importance."[5]

These brief attacks preceded the two satires devoted to the printer. *A Benevolent Epistle to Sylvanus Urban, Alias John Nichols* (1790), after a listing of the subjects of Peter Pindar's previous satires, mentions Nichols's reaction to his verse by a series of questions to his muse:

> With anger foaming and of vengeance full,
> Why belloweth John Nichols like a bull?
> Say, Goddess, could a few poetic stripes
> Make John, so furious, kick about his types;
> Spin round his Pandemonium like a Top,
> And, thundering, to its centre shake the Shop?
> Could Satire's twig produce so dire a din? (ll. 73–79)

Briefly, Peter Pindar employs the technique used in the *Epistle to the Reviewers;* he never said John Nichols wasn't honest, but then he doesn't know if his honesty stems from principle or from fear of imprisonment. He often defended the man by declaring it wasn't Nichols's fault that nature gave him a pigmy's mind. Trying to be just, he declares that no one should deride the meanest mind; after all, a horse must often guide one in the dark. In fact, Lady Truth sometimes visits the man; but Nichols cannot hear Reason's voice, for he still damns Peter's verses even though Peter is kinder to Nichols's publications: "Yet though thou *frown'st* on Peter's every line,/ Behold the difference, John! he smiles on thine" (ll. 123–24).

Nichols, told that people in glass houses should not throw stones, is asked to stop his swinelike conduct; and he is requested to imitate the mild-mannered poet, Peter Pindar. Though the satirist admits he may have been severe with Johnson's biographers, Nichols's response was out of proportion to reason, unless Nichols is jealous of Peter's success. Though attacked by Nichols, Peter has refused to claw,

> The drooping leaves of thy sad Magazine;
> Touch'd not *thy* trash, nor Hayley's tinsel stuff;
> Nor fresh, stale, *new antiquities* of Gough:
> Indeed, I'm tender-conscienced on that score,
> And learn to look with *pity* on the *poor*:
> No Mohawk I, in scenes of horror bred;
> I scorn to scalp the dying or the dead. (ll. 226–32)

Glancing through the magazine, Pindar has noticed Nichols's lack of discrimination, for a pin seems to be as important as a pyramid: "On every theme alike *his* pompous art;/ The General Conflagration or a F——" (ll. 263–64).

After claiming that Nichols tries to shove his own friends into the House of Fame, Peter again mentions Nichols's *Biographical and Literary Anecdotes of William Bowyer;* Peter says the work lacks merit and tells Nichols "Thou gavest of Bowyer's Life a Gossip's Story,/And only rear'dst a Dunghill to thy glory" (ll.293–94). Often the satirist wished to reprimand the man, but Pity said "Expose not childhood that deserves a tear;/ Set not the roaring Lion at a Rat,/ Nor call down Thunder to destroy a Gnat" (ll. 326–28). Nichols should not complain when the poet calls him the silliest man in town just because Nichols's equals can be found. He never said that hirelings wrote Nichols's works, for he knows "*all* the *blunders* of the Books are thine" (l. 340). Closing with advice cautioning Nichols not to write on history, painting, music, or anything that requires thought, he tells the publisher that, if he must write biography, he should write on the giants of Guildhall.

John Nichols did not bother to reply, so Peter Pindar wrote what purports to be Sylvanus Urban's response in *A Rowland for an Oliver* (1790). As might be expected, Nichols's voice inadvertently damns him in his own defense. In the prose preface, Nichols speaks of his own character in an attempt to win audience approval; but Peter guides the pen. Nichols mentions his own ignorance when he first became interested in antiquarian pursuits; he thought "Aug." on a coin meant the month and that Romulus and Remus were two children milking a cow. Many items, such as pig rings presented as nose jewelry, were passed off upon him, and he accepted them at face value. "In my Obituary, too, I made great mistakes, from imposition; as I gave the deaths of many that were not dead, and others that never existed. Sometimes the wickedness of Correspondents were such, that I have perpetuated the death of Bull-dogs, Greyhounds, Mastiffs, Horses, Hogs, etc. in my Obituary, under the idea that they were People of Consequence." All his antiquarian knowledge he owes to Richard Gough, who was an ignorant and illiterate fellow only a few years ago. However, to the point at hand he must come: he wrote the following poem in two hours and then decided to allow Peter Pindar to hang himself by printing some of the satirist's verses which had not been pre-

viously published. In this manner, John Wolcot was able to expand
the satire by including some of his old poems.

Pindar's "A Poetical Answer to Mister Peter Pindar's Benevolent
Epistle to John Nichols" is an attempt in doggerel verse in which
Nichols must unconsciously reveal himself. Speaking directly to
the satirist, Nichols's supposed answer begins,

> Oh Son of wicked Satan, with a Soul
> Hot as his Hell, and blacker than his Coal!
> Thou false, thou foul-mouth'd censurer of the times,
> I do not care three straws for all thy Rhymes. (ll. 1–4)

He does not fear the satirist, for he knows the best people, and no
one has ever invited Peter to his house. He employs such geniuses
as Hayley, Gough, Walpole, Anna Seward, Yeardsley, and Hannah
More to work for him. He believes Peter is angry because Nichols
"let no Author see the house of Fame,/ Before he gets a passport
in my name" (ll. 91–92). "But let my soul be calm: it sha'n't be
said/I fear thee, O thou Monster! 'Who's afraid'" (ll. 95–96).
Nichols's conclusion reveals his stupidity, his pride, and his fear
of Peter's animosity:

> Whene'er I die, I hope that I shall read
> This honest Epitaph upon my head:—
> "Here lies John's Body; but his Soul is seen
> In that famed work, the Gemman's Magazine:
> Brave, yet possess'd od all thr softer feelings;
> Successful with the Muses in his dealings;
> Mild, yet in Virtue's cause as quick as tinder—
> Who never car'd one f— for Peter Pindar." (ll. 183–90)

The remainder of this pamphlet is a collection of miscellaneous
pieces by Peter Pindar, but one deals with Nichols's book *Pro-
gresses and Public Processions of Queen Elizabeth,* written with
Gough's assistance in 1788. "To Mr. J. Nichols on his History of
the Progress of Queen Elizabeth" states that this theme is too high
for the man who should write "On somewhat on a level with thy
wit:/ For instance, when Her Majesty *made water*" (ll. 7–8).

"The Praise of Anecdote," a prose piece in *Pindariana* (1794),
pokes fun at the compilers of anecdotes of famous persons. In
addition to the life of Bowyer, Nichols had published *A Collection
of Royal and Noble Wills, with Notes and a Glossary* (1760) and

Biographical Anecdotes of Mr. Hogarth, and a Catalogue of His Works, with Occasional Remarks (1781). In this prose piece, Peter damns such endeavors by pretending they are works of value and substance: "Blessed be the *retailers* of Anecdote, who afford so much pleasant and light food to the mind. Blessed more particularly be Master John Nichols, compiler of the Magazine of *quality*," and his wonderful friend Richard Gough. "Important is the most trivial Anecdote of an *extraordinary* person; and when consecrated by age, it becomes invaluable." Furthermore, "The smallest anecdote of a man of *consequence* adds a Gem to the Treasures of History." All this paraphernalia, however, introduces a poem which has nothing to do with John Nichols.

John Nichols may have had a form of revenge upon the satirist, for his *Literary Anecdotes of the Eighteenth Century* (1817–31) only indexes Peter Pindar in connection with William Gifford and recounts the satirist's caning in Wright's bookstore.

III *The* British Critic

The *British Critic,* which began publication in May, 1793, did not deal too kindly with Peter Pindar's pamphlets; and Wolcot attacked the periodical through references to individuals associated with the magazine. Francis Rivington (1745–1822) and his brother Charles (1754–1831) began publishing this monthly periodical in 1793, and it soon reached a monthly circulation of thirty-five hundred copies. The magazine perhaps owed its success to its early editors, William Beloe (1756–1817) and his friend Robert Nares (1753–1829), who were Anglican priests as well as writers. Beloe's works, in part, consist of *Poems and Translations* (1788), *Miscellanies, Consisting of Poems, Classical Extracts, and Oriental Analogues* (1795), and such translations as *The Rape of Helen, from the Greek of Coluthus* (1786), *Alciphron's Epistles* (1791), *The History of Herodotus* (1791), and *The Attic Nights of Aulus Cellius* (1795). In addition to aiding Beloe with the fifteen volumes of *A New and General Biographical Dictionary* (1798–1816), Robert Nares wrote *Elements of Orthoepy, Containing the Whole Analogy of English Language, so Far as it Relates to Pronunciation* (1784) and *General Rules for the Pronunciation of the English Language* (1792).

In themselves, the works of these men did not arouse Peter Pindar's wrath so much as did the review of his own *Nil Admirari* in the

British Critic for November, 1799 (547–48). The review began, "It is the remark, not only of critics, but of the public at large, that the talents of Peter Pindar, such as they are, have long been on the decline and latterly have appeared to be almost exhausted. The present publication exhibits their complete extinction, and will probably fall as dead from the press, as if it had not the head of the author prefixed, or the name of a Bishop on the title-page." After applauding Bishop Porteus's judgment of Hannah More's works, the reviewer returned to Peter's satire to conclude that "There is nothing we could extract from this performance with any benefit or satisfaction to our readers, and therefore we dismiss it without further notice" (548).

John Wolcot answered these statements in the "Postscript" to *Lord Auckland's Triumph* (1800). By stating what he has not done, a method he has used before, he damns the editors and publishers of the periodical. Why, Peter asks, should the *British Critic* attack him? "Have I been known to attack Parson Nares' still-born, pious, prose Lucubrations, or Beloe's Rhymes? I scorn to insult the *dead.*—Have I ever spoken *disrespectfully* of the *critical sagacity* of Messieurs Rivingtons (two Booksellers of St. Paul's Church-Yard) and their *reviewing* Ladies? I scorn to trample on *paralytics.*"

The Horrors of Bribery (1803), dealing with an attempt of a man to purchase the office of Landing Surveyor of Plymouth, mentions the prevalence of offering money to obtain favors and refers to the men associated with the *British Critic*. Reverend Nares is "*great* in *evangelical* Children, called Sermons, poor still-born brats," while Reverend Beloe is "*great* in *literary* Children, long since *dead,* named Translation, Poems, etc." These two men "sit on the *apex* of Parnassus, and *dispose* of *places* to literary Ladies and Gentlemen who sigh for a niche in the temple of Immortality. As criticism is considered by the aforesaid *gentlemen* in the light of a *trade,* like *bookselling* and *preaching,* they naturally endeavor to *make the most of it.*"[6] These two are also castigated in a footnote by being presented as men who pay for the scalps of authors; Peter, furthermore, questions their piety: "To be somewhat serious; I would advise these two *reviewing parsons,* who pretend to piety and morals, not to damn a little amatory line in *one* Author, and recommend in a stream of panegyric a work that would have defied the prurient powers of the famous Lord Rochester to surpass."[7]

Tristia (1806) contains the last of the satirist's complaints about the publishers, but they are numerous. The "Elegy to the Bat" speaks of this "imp of night" who battles harmless creatures and thus reminds Peter Pindar of Parson Nares "Who, when young Genius his light wing prepares,/ Leaps from the shop of Rivington to kill it" (ll. 11–12). The reviews of this magazine are quite deadly, for there is not one "that doth not cast a blight;/That does not try to murder every Muse./And cloud her merits with oblivious night" (ll. 17–20). That bat murders for food to live, but Nares murders to gain luxury, and thus Pindar learns that "Critics, like Demons, thrive upon *Damnation*" (1. 32).

In the "Elegy to Mr. Sheridan," after noting that the playwright and Member of Parliament has been successful in life, Pindar becomes personal in stating that reviewers are worse than Peter. He himself has reviewed books but not like the *British Critic*'s reviewers: "Merit with *Tomahawks* I ne'er pursued;/ *Spared* hooting *owls,* and *kill'd* the birds of *song*" (ll. 15–16). Yet Rivington's reviews caused him much anguish, but then he is "Poor Orpheus 'midst the Bacchanalian throng" (1. 24). He believes that Beloe, Nares, Thomas Rennell (1787–1824), who became editor of the *British Critic* in 1811, and Thomas Maurice (1754–1824), a voluminous writer on historical and Oriental subjects, are responsible for attacks on him; and his opinion is that some stinking weeds have stolen the name of the flower of genius. Actually, he could find such men as they anywhere, Rennels by the gross, and "*Thousands* of Nares, and Maurices, and Beloes" (1. 52).

In the "Elegy to Mr. Rowlandson," Peter exclaims that, if he possessed the power of Rowlandson's pen, he would draw these priests in a pillory on Parnassus and have them begging for mercy while the Muses throw rotten eggs. He embellishes the imaginary caricature by adding two figures which express his low opinion of the *British Critic*; Hypocrisy, the only mourner, drops the journal "Its *leaden* leaves by Taste and Genius torn" (1. 15); and Aristarchus points to them with contempt, crying, "The *foes* of Learning who have *stolen* my chair" (1. 20).

The last comment, in "Elegy to a Friend," reveals how the poet obtained his small library, an ironical way to deal with his enemies:

> *Subscribing* to a Chandler's Shop for *cheese,*
> I gain the labour; of celestial thought:
> Sermons of Nares my eye with wonder sees,
> And reads his British Critic all for *nought*   (ll. 5–8)

IV Booksellers

The comments on John Nichols of the *Gentlemen's Magazine* and on the Rivingtons of the *British Critic* illustrate that Wolcot held critics and printers in low repute, and he added booksellers to this list but with a different emphasis. An "Ode,"[8] found in *Pindariana* (1794), stresses the idea that booksellers, uncreative themselves, are tradesmen who drive hard bargains: for example, Milton was only paid fifteen pounds for *Paradise Lost*. Too many rhymers and historians have heard them ask a writer how long it took to produce the work, as if he were to be paid by the hour. So angered is Pindar by this thought that he castigates them collectively by calling them a beast which hasn't a single portion of the fire of writers and can't learn from them: "Rolls not thine eye upon their Works each day?/And canst thou from them *nothing* bear away,/ To lift thy hog-like soul above the mire?" (ll. 22–24). The booksellers simply cannot recognize that content should be more valued than the number of pages in a work. They are like the country bumpkin who complained over the one-shilling charge to have a tooth extracted. The bumpkin protests because the extraction took but half a minute; previously, Dr. Slop had dragged him three times about the shop for the same price. Obviously, Peter implies booksellers, like bumpkins, do not understand nor appreciate skill and talent.

Though the lines in "Peter's Triumph," the concluding poem of *Tears and Smiles* (December, 1801) refer to himself, they reveal Wolcot's general views about booksellers, as his biographers will attest. In this poem the satirist brags, boasts, and complains while he speaks to his muse about the niggardliness of booksellers:

> Muse, we have finish'd now our Odes,
> And verily the Songs of Gods;
> But let me tell thee, Muse (and much it pains,)
> That those great traffikers in *words*,
> Those high and mighty pompous Lords,
> The Booksellers, will barely give me *grains*.
>
> "*Hogs' wash* is good enough," they cry:
> Thus can I neither roast nor fry.   (ll.1–8)

His mind is forced to grind flour for them while he, himself, feeds on bran. They drink claret and burgundy from his skull and tell

him to be happy with small dead beer. Only one thought makes his
existence bearable: "*My* name never will be forgotten:/When to
Posterity I make my bow,/These rogues are in oblivion rotten"
(ll. 23–24).

The above lines may have been written because of the lawsuit
which Wolcot brought against his publishers when they stopped his
annuity. This situation, however, seems to be more clearly expressed
in the concluding lines of *The Island of Innocence* (May, 1802):

> Fired with the love of Rhyme, and let me say,
> Of Virtue too, I pour'd the moral Lay.
> Much like Saint Paul (who solemnly protests
> He battled hard at Ephesus with *beasts*),
> I've fought with lions, monkeys, bulls, and bears,
> And got half Noah's ark about my ears;
> Nay *worse* (which all the Courts of Justice know)
> Fought with the *brutes* of Paternoster-Row.

As pointed out in Chapter 1, Wolcot wanted independence;
only money could assure it. Thus his anger in connection with booksellers may be suspect. It may be true that the booksellers did not
recognize the value of a work of art and that they considered bulk
to be the important aspect of a manuscript and paid accordingly;
but the satirist seems to want to have much money paid him for
slim pamphlets that he claims booksellers cannot in any case evalu-
ate. It is understandable, however, that he wants money; it does
exactly what Wolcot knew it did—secured independence. If Wolcot
appears to be greedy, it must be remembered that booksellers are
also partly to blame—they do act like businessmen. Wolcot is at
least correct in saying that his name is not forgotten and that no one
remembers the names of the booksellers.

CHAPTER 6

Thomas Paine and the French Revolution

JOHN Wolcot's 1760–61 sojourn in France produced within him a decided antipathy toward all things French.[1] With the beginning of French Revolution in 1789, he was quite pleased to see that France might become a democratic country; but the excesses of the Revolution after 1792 tended to make him gloat over that nation's self-ruin. The works of Thomas Paine (1737–1809) which criticized England produced on Wolcot's part the pose of the patriotic Englishmen who sees his liberty as possibly threatened from abroad; yet it was the legislative acts beginning in 1792, passed by the British government to curb sedition and treason, which made the satirist perceive that liberty was endangered at home. These acts, the government's reaction to Paine and to the French Revolution, made Wolcot most angry; and they account for his references to loss of liberty in his poetry. In this connection Peter Pindar protested that he was no enemy of the king or of the government but only a corrector of faults found in the government's representatives. In Pindar's satires, then, one may trace Wolcot's views toward France, Thomas Paine, and the French Revolution—views amplified in those satires about William Pitt and George III.

This group of satires also illustrates the anti-French and anti-Catholic prejudices which colored Peter Pindar's outlook and his style and which resulted in some coarse material in a satire. What is evident in this group is that the tone in his *Epistle to the Pope,* expressing anger that the Pope has not attacked France, is far different from his other satires. When Wolcot dealt with French political events, he evinced a definite tendency for his voice to sound extremely serious when giving advice, and such seriousness produced prosaic satires. Metrically, they are verse; but, in terms of metaphor and structure, they seem merely prose sentences and statements. Irony, exaggeration, and rhyme are here but are unaccompanied by good-humored wit.

One element in Peter Pindar's method not so frequently illustrated before in this study is the use of the tale or fable. When the poet compares himself to Thomas Paine in "The Magpie and the Robin Red-Breast" or when be offers tyrants some advice in the tales of "The Candle and the Pin" and "The Sun and the Peacock," Peter Pindar skillfully and humorously makes his point or amplifies it; but, when these tales are brought in merely to extend the length of a satire and have little bearing on the satire itself, he often fails to interest or amuse the reader. Most of the tales used are taken from Aesop and La Fontaine, but the best ones are those which John Wolcot himself created. Wolcot's tales, however, exhibit the most brilliance when they deal with human beings and when the basis for the story is a true incident related to some famous person, as in "The Applie Dumplings and the King." For this reason they are really an extension of the poet's topical satire, a report in verse.

Furthermore, that Wolcot wished to write serious poetry is evident in the works about Thomas Paine and the French Revolution; but the flashes of brilliance, the skillful use of metaphor, and the fresh use of imagery are not exhibited in his serious pieces. which seem so similar to other eighteenth-century poems by less skilled poets that one almost suspects that they were not written by John Wolcot. They are conventional in subject matter, treatment, and sentiments. The only poem that has some vitality is the "Ode to Innocence"; and, significantly, it is perhaps an unintended parody on such eighteenth-century poems to the maid who is Innocence personified; only here Wolcot seems to break out of the pattern and to express his true feelings. To state what he really felt and to mock good-naturedly what he disapproved of made Peter Pindar's mind active and stimulated him to produce his best and most lively work.

Wolcot's abilities must not, however, be overemphasized; the satires examined in this chapter reveal his mundane qualities and even call into question his defense of a cause. His animosity toward the French seems to have stemmed from a personal pique suffered when he lived in that country for a year; he wished to see France suffer and fail. He was becoming personally involved when, as he saw government legislative measures threaten liberty at home, he used satire as a weapon to combat such acts. Yet his lines most frequently seem strident, and mellowness is absent. In terms of Peter Pindar's satires, these poems do not rank high; in terms of his ability as a writer, they reflect a decline. Politics and political situations, as the next chapter about English politicians reveals, was not the area in which the satirist exhibited himself to the best of his ability.

I *Attacks on France*

"Ode XIV" of the *Lyric Odes to the Royal Academicians for 1785* illustrates the satirist's antipathy toward French customs and manners. After stating that the unrealistic works of French artists are standing jokes, Peter Pindar becomes autobiographical while stressing his critical "impartiality":

> Think not I wantonly the French attack
> I never will put MERIT on the rack:
> No; yet, I own, I hate the shrugging dogs.
> I've lived among them, eat their frogs,
> And vomited them up, thank God, again:
>   So that I'm able now to say,
>   I carried nought of *theirs* away,
> Which otherwise had made the Puppies *vain*.   (ll. 29–36)

No biography of the satirist reveals the reason for Wolcot's hatred, but French manners may have been the cause. "Bien-séance" in *Subjects for Painters* (1789) finds the French inclined to this word which Peter says means keeping a smooth face when one is kicked. If used correctly, "bien-séance" stands in place of something solid, but can lead to Folly as the story of "The Petit Maitre and the Man on the Wheel" reveals. In it, Peter presents the public chastisement of a German law breaker who, when placed on the wheel, roars out at each stroke of the lash. A passing *"petit-maître"* tells him that it is contrary to "Bien-séance" for him to make such a noise. Wolcot apparently felt that certain manners and attitudes of the French were unrealistic and that reason should govern a man and his actions.

Since Pindar's attitudes toward the monarchy are closely allied to his views on France, they should be examined. In his *Expostulatory Odes* (1789), he clarified his views about any monarchy even though he had the English throne primarily in mind. He merely wishes to correct evils which he sees existing in the king and to point out their faults to individuals blinded by the trappings of royalty. In "Ode XI," he states he won't flatter a king—he won't be a bug crawling on a monarch's back. In Asia, kings are deemed heavenly creatures and people crouch before them, but this position is too servile for him. When he first came to London,

> I own I brought two *wondering* eyes to town:
> Got bent by mobs my Ribs like any Hoop,
> To see the might Man who wore a Crown;
> To see the man to whom great Courtiers stoop. (ll. 25–28)

By gaping and staring, he found that his admiration gradually disappeared, and he could view these exalted beings without emotion as human creatures. His earlier view that Jove formed kings from special cloth and common folks from scraps was changed. Because of this altered attitude, he cannot give kings even a thimbleful of praise.

The Rights of Kings (1791), dealing with the fact that Thomas Laurence, despite the king's wishes, was not made a member of the Royal Academy, declares that royal prerogatives are lost. The French Assembly, claims "Ode II," will laugh at the loss; but "Ode VIII" points out that modern Frenchmen believe a monarch must be well secured or guarded. "Ode XV" informs the reader that idolatry is dead, that the Virtues sleep, and that opposition is on the rise. Such is the case with Louis of France since the Bastille is now no more. Ironically, Peter Pindar says that people should cherish royalty which can dispense favors. These playful attitudes soon changed, however, as a result of Thomas Paine's influence.

II *Thomas Paine*

When Edmund Burke published *Reflections on the French Revolution* (1790) arguing for evolutionary rather than revolutionary change, Thomas Paine replied with Part I of *The Rights of Man* (March, 1791) criticizing the English social and economic system.[2] Paine's work, including Part II of *The Rights of Man* (February, 1792),[3] was somewhat responsible for the government's suppression of liberal societies and for the Bill of 1792 prohibiting "the writing, printing, selling, and circulating of seditious publications."[4] The French Revolution gave impetus to the reform movement in England: the Society for Constitutional Information was revived in 1791; the Corresponding Society to encourage constitutional discussion began operation in January, 1792; and the Society of Friends of the People was formed in April, 1792.[5] Public opinion soon changed, and, after Part II of Paine's *Rights of Man* appeared, Paine was regarded as an enemy by many of the people. W.E. Woodward points out the widespread fear of Paine and his writings: "Bonfires were made of his books, not merely in a few places but all over England; and images of Paine himself made of straw were burned at numerous stakes planted on village greens and at country crossroads."[6] Medals were even struck off exhibiting the author on a gibbet.[7] Paine's publisher was charged with printing and circulating seditious literature, and Paine fled from England. Tried in absentia on December 18, 1793, Thomas Paine was found guilty of high treason and thus became an outlaw in England and in all British dominions.[8] Although the government engaged in a great deal of activity searching for seditious and treasonous publications and individuals, John Wolcot was never among those considered dangerous to the state.

Angry at Paine's suggestion in *The Rights of Man* that other nations should follow France's example, John Wolcot wrote *Odes to Mr. Paine* (July, 1791). Opening with pretended admiration of Paine's vast endeavor, Peter Pindar then wonders why the book was written and suggests that Paine felt that too much peace existed in the world. It seemed shameful that Britain was happy when the rest of the globe wasn't: "How dares the Wren amidst his hedges sing,/While Eagles droop the beak, and flag the wing?" (ll. 11-12). Paine had traveled to France in March, 1791; but he returned in July of the same year.[9] Peter wonders why the man crept secretively away and bids him return to open the jails and become the leader of the inmates. Comparing himself to Paine, Peter wonders why he thought himself daring to strike at royal foibles:

> Importance, in a nut-shell hide thy head!
> *I* deem's myself a Dare-devil in Rhyme;
> To *whisper* to a King of modern time,
>   And try to strike a Royal *foible* dead:
>   While dauntless *thou* of treason makest no bones,
>   But strikest at *Kings themselves* upon their Thrones. (ll. 37–42)

The picture of Paine as mob leader is imaginatively amplified in "Ode II" when Hell hears the prayers of Paine and the jails and the insane asylums open their doors. Concluding the poem with a "Song by Mr. Paine," Peter Pindar pictures the man as a roustabout who attacks law and order. This image is created through the words

of the song supposedly written by Mr. Paine as he gives a toast to
Confusion and to success to the cause "As we've nothing to lose, lo,
nought can be lost;/So perdition to Monarchs and Laws!" (ll. 3–4).
France has shown the world the great example; and, since Paine's
followers are poor, it is quite right "At the doors of the rich ones
to thunder;/ Like the Thieves who set fire to a dwelling by night,/
And come in for a share of the plunder" (ll. 10-12). Continuing
his song, Paine argues that Britain has had peace for too long a
time and it wouldn't matter if the revolutionists failed; they would
all go to Hell together in triumph.

   The Remonstrance (October, 1791) soon followed; and in it
Peter defends himself against the charge that he had joined the
king's party just because he had attacked Paine. He attacks court
foibles, not the throne; and he detests revolutionaries, who are
designated by a tavern where many of them meet and who are as
destructive and as useful as tares (weeds):

> Again, ye Crown-and-Anchor Sinners,
> I reprobate your Revolution Dinners.
> Nature at times makes wretched wares,
> Among the smiling Corn like Tares:
>   Men with such miserable souls,
> Nought pleases, from the moment of their birth;
> With horror for a while they blot the Earth,
>   Then Crab-like crawl into their Burying holes.   (ll. 147–54)

Addressing the revolutionists, Pindar turns physician and diagnoses
their mania as a result of an inflammation of the brain which the
jails or the stocks would cure. He then gloats over France's condition
by applying the metaphor of the ship of state to that country:

> Keel up lies France: long may she keep that posture!
> Her knavery, folly, on the rocks have toss'd her,
>   Behold the thousands that surround the wreck!
> Her cables parted, rudder gone,
> Split all her sails, her main-mast down,
>   Choak'd all her pumps, broke in her deck;
>   Sport for the winds, the billows o'er her roll.—
> Now am I glad of it with all my soul.   (ll. 183–90)

France, says the poet, is Britain's Carthage. He who loves a Frenchman wars with nature, for one does not take a snake to his bosom.

Peter hates the French because they are foes of friendship and of beauty; their hearts are dunghills feeding weeds. How, he questions, can the French be called wise for dragging down a pyramid without having a pebble to replace it? Yes, he hates the French who are "Only a larger kind of Monkey"(l. 242).

To this poem, Wolocot adds a fable, one of the poet's best devices when properly used. The tale, "The Magpie and the Robin Red-Breast," was so highly admired by the *Gentleman's Magazine* (October, 1791) that it was quoted in its entirety in the magazine's poetry section. The magpie, resting on a castle turret after its journey from France, notices a robin in a bush below, and suggests that they join together in rioting and cursing the great. They should make London dance, "Not steal *unknown*, like Cukoos, to our graves,/ But imitate the Geniuses of France" (ll. 61–62). When the Robin protests that he cannot see the fun in engaging in such practices which border on damnation, the magpie tells him not to worry since France has abolished religion and views Christ as only a man. Shuddering at such a "cursed doctrine" (1.96), the robin refuses to join the blackbird; so the magpie flies off, and the robin returns to his simple sweet song. The satirist, pointing out the moral of the tale that was written because he had been asked to join a revolutionary society,[10] says, "In Thomas Paine the Magpie doth appear:/ That I'm poor Robin, is *not quite so clear"* (ll. 103–4).

Odes to Kien Long (November, 1792), addressed to the emperor of China, speaks, in "Ode II," of the distance between the king and his subjects. Most thrones are too high; therefore, French subjects are setting up ladders to come closer to kings. Rebels now wish to bridle kings, and one need only observe the practice of the wicked French who would use royal robes to wipe their shoes. Frenchmen say they want no more pickpockets as rulers and that the very dustman is superior to nobility in glittering carriages. Religion is even in a decline there, and religious relics are treated as if they were pieces of rotten timber. The public no longer sees merit in birth and thinks virtues have left the palace.

The "Ode to Messiurs Townsend, Macmanus, and Jealous, the Thief-takers and Attendents on his Majesty" deals with the anger and the dread which the name of Thomas Paine produced and with the poet's fear that civil liberties will be endangered. He advises the sedition hunters to guard the door against the author of *The Rights of Man*: "Tom Paine's an artful and rebellious dog;/

Swears that a *sacred* Throne is but a Log,/ And Monarchs *too expensive* to maintain" (ll. 24-26). Because Tom Paine is "A name of fear that sounds in every wind;/ A Goblin damn'd that haunts the Royal mind;/ Of Damocles the hair-suspended Sword" (ll.29–31), their majesties sleep badly at night. Peter claims that informers tell the king stories that surpass the tales about Robin Hood, and he concludes that monarchs in days gone by trusted in a people's love and not Bow-street runners.

Pindariana (1794) depicts Paine as the foe of law, order, and religion in the "Hymn to the Guillotine":

> Oh let us view thy *lofty* grace!
> To Briton's shew thy *blushing* face,
>   And bless Rebellion's *life-tired* train. —
> Joy to my soul! she's on her way,
> Led by her *dearest* friends, Dismay,
>   Death, and the Devil, and Tom Paine.   (ll. 13–18)

The last reference to Paine occurs in Canto III of "Orson and Ellen; A Legendary Tale" found in *Tears and Smiles* (1801). Boniface, a tavern owner, and Orson, a traveler, turn their conversation to Dame Religion; and both agree that in France her pockets were picked, her clothes stolen, and her reputation maligned since the French claimed she was a friar's bastard, as well as a hypocrite and a liar to her children. France also stole her jewels and destroyed the saints's relics and statues. The talk then turns to Peter Pindar, and Orson says some people thought the satirist was as bad as Tom Paine, a man whose books were burned and whom the people had wanted to burn along with the books.

III Freedom and Tyranny

France's success in her wars prompted Peter to advise Pope Pius VI in *A Poetical, Serious and Possibly Impertinent Epistle to the Pope* (July, 1793), a work which also exhibits the satirist's anti-Catholic feelings. The Pope is reprimanded because he has done nothing to stop the advance of France who "for Freedom mad, invades thy rights,/ And pours her Millions o'er the World like Mites" (ll. 1–2). While France threatens Sardinia and Naples, "Where is th' Almighty's *man*, the Church's Hope,/ Prince of Salvation, Peter's Heir, the Pope?" (ll. 11–12). Peter condemns the pope for not even issuing a papal bull against France. The power of the saints, the satirist says, was once great; but the pope appears to have forgotten about this power:

> Hear with what *blasphemy* this France behaves!
> "Rome, I despise thee: all thy Popes are Knaves;
> Thy Cardinal; and Priests the earth encumber;
> Avaunt the Saints, and all such *holy lumber*!
> . . . .
> *Saint* Jail, *Saint* Whip, *Saint* Guillotine, *Saint* Rope,
> Posses (we think) more virtue than the Pope.   (ll. 65–80)

France will no longer feed the priests, will melt the silver saints into coins, and will even find a way to make the charms of nuns useful. France claims that the masses said for the departed soul never put out a single fire in hell. The intentions of the French, says Peter, show that Reason has escaped from bondage and claims the range of Heaven. All these ideas illustrate that infidelity exists abroad, and the satirists asks if the French should go unpunished. The heir of Saint Peter should attack these people, use his treasury for building warships, and even use saints' relics against them. All he need do is attack them, for the atheists will yield. Prayer, however, is not enough; and to illustrate the point, the satirist tells the story of "The Waggoner and Jupiter." When a wagon went into a ditch, its clodlike driver howled for aid from Jupiter. Jupiter calls the man lazy, tells him to put his shoulder to the wheel and to flog the horses, which the man does; and the wagon is soon on its way again. The poet then advises the pope to imitate this clod. Peter Pindar, unfortunately, dilutes the effect of his advice by attaching three coarse poems to this epistle. One suggests that, when the pope was a friar, he kept a mistress; the second presents a whorehouse madam who, on her deathbed, wonders what the young man who has just requested her services will do when she is with her Lord in Heaven; and the third, "Ode to Innocence," is only delightful as a parody of eighteenth-century odes on personified abstractions.

As previously stated, John Wolcot often expanded the number of pages in a satire by including material which did not specifically pertain to his main subject. The "Ode to Innocence" is such a poem; and, though it does not pertain to France, it is discussed now since it was included in a work mentioning France. The primary reason for its treatment here, however, is that it is a far better

poem than the *Epistle to the Pope* and contains a sentiment concerning passion which frequently occurs in the satirist's work. Peter
begins with a description of the sensibilities of this maid known as
"Innocence": she is a wanderer in rural areas and hates the city;
she pities the fly used to catch fish; and she spends her time observing
the bee, the ant, the butterfly, and the wren's nest. He, the poet,
pleased with her and her activities, could sit by her side and listen
to the sounds of grazing sheep. A typical poem would have closed
on this note of rural bliss, but Peter Pindar turns to present a
different call of nature, revealing that the simple country life is not
really for him. After the poet repeats the simple pleasures found
with "Innocence," he then adds:

> Thus could I dwell with thee for many an hour:—
> Yet *should* a rural Venus from her bow'r
>   Step forth with bosom bare, and beaming eye,
> And flaxen locks, luxuriant rose-clad cheek,
> And purple lip, and dimpled chin so sleek,
>   And archly heave the love-seducing sigh;
>
> And cry, "Come hither, Swain; be not afraid:
> Embrace the *wild*, and quit the *simple* Maid:"—
>   I *verily* believe that I should *go*:
> Yet parting should I say to thee, "Farewell;
> I cannot help it; witchcraft's in her cell,
>   The Passions like to be where tempests blow.
> "Go, Girl, enjoy thy Fish, and Flies, and Doves;
> But suffer *me* to giggle with the Loves."
>
> Thus should I act. Excuse me, charming Saint:
> An imp am I, in Virtue's cause so faint;
>   Like David in his youth, a lawless swain:
> Preferring (let me own with blushing face)
> The *storms* of Passion to the *calms* of Grace;
>   One *ounce* of Pleasure to a *pound* of Pain.   (ll. 45–65)

The use of comparison and contrast, plus the precise descriptive
detail, heightens the comic effect of the poem. However, the poem
questions Peter Pindar's sincerity for a cause. By adding extraneous
material to his satire, Wolcot has only weakened the effect of his
attack upon France and the pope.

    John Wolcot's pride in the British system of government did not
extend to its repressive acts, and his view that monarchs are human

beings brings him close to treasonable utterances in the "Ode to Tyrants," one of the *Pathetic Odes* (1794):

> Who, and *what* are ye, sceptred Bullies, speak,
> That millions to *your* will must bow the neck,
>   And, Ox-like, meanly take the galling yoke?
> Philosophers your ignorance despise;
> Even Folly laughing lifts her maudlin eyes,
>   And freely on your *Wisdoms* cracks her joke.
>
> How dare ye on the Man of Labour tread,
> Whose honest toils supply your mouths with bread: (ll. 1–8)

Monarchs are not sent by God; they have no credentials. So Peter Pindar suggests that men really are responsible for the election of rulers whom they are stupid enough to respect; it would make one laugh to see a tailor bow to the satin breeches which he has made. An "Ode"[11] states that all kings think their makers, the people, are slaves, an idea which makes kings either fools or villains. These great people think that honors were made for them and that their makers are mere mob and dirt.

Two fables are used to illustrate what kings owe to their subjects. "The Diamond Pin and the Farthing Candle. A Fable" deals with a vain pin (king), proud of her sparkle, who tells the candle (common man) to keep its distance. The candle informs the pin that she shines only by the candle's light, and at that moment the maid blows out the candle. When asked where her radiance is now, the pin admits that she has mistaken her own nature. The candle says the pin should reverence the blaze, the creator, and not herself. In "The Sun and the Peacock. A Fable," the bird proclaims her tail is more beautiful than the sun. When the sun withdraws behind a cloud, the beauty of the peacock's feather eyes is gone. Realizing its folly, the peacock asked that it be allowed to shine again. Peter Pindar adds that, if the tyrants of Eastern realms cannot discover the meaning of these two fables, they had better learn soon before their subjects teach them the message.

Peter Pindar's sentimental vein and his serious attempts as a poet are revealed in some of the minor pieces of *Pindariana* (1794). Though these poems are not satires, a few deal with France and illustrate some of Wolcot's feelings toward that country. "The Captive Queen. The Lines are supposed to be spoken by a Friend of the unfortunate Antoinette" was, no doubt, a suitable topic for sentiment during the period. In this poem, the "friend" says that the voice of joy is now mute, pity soothes the queen's sorrows, but hope must no longer charm the ear. What is life, the friend wonders, when murder and horror reign? She tells the queen that her fame will outlast time itself, but the forthcoming blow will put her virtues in the tomb.

"The Queen of France to Her Children, just before Her Execution. An Elegiac Ballad" presents a resigned Antoinette who informs her brood that she goes with joy from the prison since the grave holds no terror. Asking her children to gather around her, she blesses them: and she hopes by her death that the cloud hanging over them will be dispersed and reveal only sunshine for them. Both poems reveal some maudlin sentimentality on the poet's part, and what effect they have upon the reader is based not on the poetry but upon the reader's knowledge of Antoinette's life and death.

In *Pindariana*, Peter Pindar becomes slightly angry with Jacques Delille (1738–1813), a French poet who was briefly imprisoned in France. In the "Ode to the Poet Delille," Wolcot is pleased that the man has been released from the dungeon in which Robespierre had imprisoned him; but he adds that Delille will now probably praise the convention of France and say that Britain will cower before it. Peter requests that the English be spared this propaganda. Delille should have more sense and should despise his country, which is a graduate of the school of hypocrisy. If Delille must vent his rage, it should fall upon the figure of justice which guides the pen of Peter Pindar.

"A Second Ode to the Poet Delille" states that reason has become a slaughterhouse and that the millions in France shout only of murder and death. Pindar advises Delille to leave his country, which has become a foe to wisdom since it went mad. "A Third Ode to the Poet Delille" presents Wolcot's view that emotionalism ruined the ideals of the French Revolution. For freedom, a nation's head was cut off; and, instead of finding freedom, it found tyranny. Madame Prudence was not there, for the people were and still are ruled by Passion; and the satirist then asks why passion was aligned against a king and a queen who had done nothing wrong.

Liberty's Last Squeak (1795) was written as a result of the British government's bills against sedition and treason—bills so far-reaching that they endangered personal liberty and freedom of speech. The Habeas Corpus Act was suspended in 1794, and in 1795 the Seditious Meetings Act limited public assemblies, while "the Treasonable Practices Act re-defined the law of treason. Those who devised evil against the king, those who plotted to help invaders, and those who sought to coerce parliament were all brought within its scope; those who dared to attack the constitution were made liable to seven years' transportation."[12] In the "Ode to an Informer," in *Liberty's Last Squeak*, Peter suggests, therefore, that people will be arrested for naming their dog Tom Paine, and the parrot which cries Paine's name will be executed. Only "God Save the King" will be allowed, and even the owl will have to learn it. Furthermore, the conditions of paupers must not be mentioned: "What Journeyman will dare to mention *wages*?/ *Who* talk about the hardships of the Poor./ Off with the Villains to their iron cages" (ll. 45–47). The Dissenters and the Jews will be shot, and the tongues of Quakers will be cut out. These legislative acts recently passed will bring back the days of the tyrants when power saw what one was thinking and crushed treasonable sighs. Yes,

> The voice of Liberty has roar'd too long:
> Pull out the wide-mouth'd strumpet's lawless tongue;
> Off with the wonted Crown that decks her head
> And place the *proper* Fool's cap in its stead.   (ll. 65–68)

The "Second Ode to an Informer" claims that night and silence aids the man in his work. Newgate and the Tower will each soon say that they are too crowded, that there is not room for a pin, and the pillory and the gibbet will groan from overwork. He bids the informer to drag the husband from his wife's nightly embrace and to imprison the drunken youth who mutters "Freedom" and "Tom Paine." The informer should knock down the man ruled by reason and thereby secure his own fortune by rope and chains.

"Ode to the French," found in *The Royal Tour* (1795), a satire on George III, states that the French who lately adored kings have treated them badly; but the French always rush to extremes and need common sense to guide them. Peter admits that, as a youth, he had thought kings owned the universe and could change things into gold; but he now sees them differently. In the same satire, in "A Hint to a Poor Democrat," he advises the man not to call the king a fool; it's impolite, even if not a lie. He should learn to speak the truth only of the devil. The democrat's passions are too much

like France's; so, to be safe, he should bow down to Pitt, the prime
minister.

    The Fall of Portugal: or the Royal Exiles. A Tragedy in Five Acts
(1808), Wolcot's serious attempt at drama, may be mentioned
here since it pertains to France. In 1807, France occupied Portugal;
and the Portuguese royal family fled to Brazil. In Wolcot's treatment
of the event, Alvarez, a courtier filled with the emotions of ambition
and revenge because he was not allowed to marry Elvira, puts his
trust in Bellegarde, the ambassador from France, and hopes to
gain revenge and empire by turning traitor to the regent of Portugal.
Alvarez, speaking of the regent, says: "And tho', he deems me
such a humble worm,/ Yet shall he feel that worm conceals a
fang" (I,ii). Of course, the Frenchman is merely using the courtier;
for Bellegarde says, "Thus Frenchmen rule by art as well as arms;/
And use Ambition, just to edge their tools" (I, ii). Wolcot engages
in some flag waving when the prince of Brazil, the regent of Portugal,
speaks of the safety which Britain can offer him from Napoleon:

> The giant power of Britain—sacred spot!—
> The fam'd asylum from despotic power;
> Where banish'd Kings and Princes find a home;
> Where reigns a sovereign in his people's hearts;
> That happy Isle, where Freedom only dwells,
> To rescue from a tyrant's rage the world.   (III, i)

Montford, the ambassador of England, gives the French ambassador
his comeuppance after a verbal exchange by stating the form
which Napoleon's blessings take:

> If famine, tyranny, and wounds, and death;
> The cries of orphans, and the widow's moans,
> That sadden every wind that blows, be blessings,
> Napoleon blesses with a bounteous hand.   (III, i)

The villain Alvarez is discovered and takes poison in prison. The
prince of Brazil leaves his country, and the last scene depicts Britain
as a protector of the weak. Act V, Scene ii, opens with a view of
the Portuguese fleet under sail, the French marching into the city,
the spectators singing a patriotic ode; and the curtain falls on the
sight of the British fleet joining that of Portugal. *The Fall of Portugal*
is extremely poor in plot and dialogue; but, with all the flag waving,

it is obvious on which side the author has placed himself. The play, however, was never staged.

Anticipation: or, The Prize Address[13] (1813) is another piece of loud patriotism, but this time spoken by Peter Puncheon, a landlord who doesn't buy French wines; only claret goes into his "patriot glass" (l. 26). If Napolean invades, "Soon the mock Monarch shall to fate be hurl'd;/ For we who hold the trident rule the world" (ll. 39–40). After toasting Britain's military leaders, Puncheon concludes with a song, "Britannia, rule the waves,/ For freeborn Britons never will be slaves!" (ll. 137–38). This patriotic piece is the least of Wolcot's productions.

John Wolcot's final reference to France occurs in his last published work, *A Most Solemn and Important Epistle to the Emperor of China* (1817). Angered that the 1816 British delegation to China had not been received at the Chinese court, Peter Pindar warns the Chinese emperor:

> Reflect, what BRITAINS can perform;
> Of FRANCE who fac'd the hostile storm,
> (France that on Realms had fix'd her tyger pats);
>   Then chain'd, his ruthless rage to mock,
>   NAPOLEON to a barren Rock—
> By all deserted but his neighbors' rats.   (ll. 157–62)

CHAPTER 7

William Pitt and Other Politicians

PRIME Minister William Pitt (1759–1806), who ably guided England through the trying period of the early wars with France (1793–1802), was attacked by John Wolcot because of his tax policies and his legislative measures designed to curb sedition and treason. In order to undermine Pitt's public position, Wolcot frequently referred to incidents in the man's life; so a brief biographical sketch of William Pitt, listing only those facts pertinent to Wolcot's satires, must be given. Throughout his lifetime Pitt suffered from a delicate constitution and drank wine to build up his strength.[1] His early introduction to wine may have led to his consuming large amounts of port, for much later in life tales were told of drunken bouts with friends, leading Henry Addington to remark at one time that Pitt liked a bottle of port more than a single glass.[2]

Pitt entered the House of Commons on January 23, 1781, as the representative of Appleby, a pocket borough controlled by James Lowther; and before Pitt was twenty-five years old, he became prime minister on December 19, 1783, a position which he held until March 14, 1801.[3] As administrator during the wars with France, Pitt inaugurated new taxes and measures to control treasonous writings and actions; Wolcot censured both of these policies. Though Pitt was an able administrator for the government, he was never able to manage his own affairs; and, when he left office, he was forty-five thousand pounds in debt—[4] a fact that disproves Wolcot's charge that the prime minister enriched himself while in office. Peter Pindar's satires against the prime minister followed the man's political career closely, and a chronological arrangement of them illuminates the background of the satires and also provides a brief history of the times.

Some of Peter Pindar's opinions of William Pitt do not coincide with the facts, as has been noted; but they reflect a portion of the feelings of the public. Pitt is regarded as leading the nation to destruction through bankruptcy because of his tax programs. The satirist regards the war with France as unnecessary since it drains the public funds and detracts from English democratic principles, for government funds are used to support tottering thrones on the Continent. Repressive measures to insure the country's safety from sedition and treason have led only to a reduction of personal liberty and curtailment of free speech. Furthermore, Pitt wanted power, perhaps even wished to take over the throne—an opinion not suported by historical fact. Pitt's fall from office is viewed as beneficial for the country; but Peter Pindar incorrectly infers that Pitt left office far richer than when he entered it.

In attacking Pitt, Peter Pindar, as usual with him, has recourse to images connected with the animal kingdom, images with which he is thoroughly at home. Pitt is seen as a dairy farmer milking dry a cow, the nation. He is a coachman using the nation as his hack, or an Alexander attempting to use the Prince of Wales as his horse. Except for these instances, there is a certain lack of wit, of invention, or of cleverness in the satires about Pitt. Perhaps Peter Pindar felt that such a subject—the bankruptcy of a nation through poor administration—necessitated serious treatment. In any case, there is a tendency, as in his other political satires, toward the prosaic which deadens the verses' effectiveness. A spark of his humorous irony is often missing which would make the lines catch fire. It may be granted that Peter Pindar was voicing a popular opinion in respect to Pitt and that he exhibited his personal feelings also, but the artist in him appears to have faltered on this subject. Perhaps it was too difficult to be whimsical and humorous when charges of sedition could be leveled against writers and publishers, the members of Wolcot's profession. In any case, Peter Pindar is more of the apostle-preacher than the poet-humorist. With political satire, his work most closely approaches the manner of other satirists of his period and lacks, therefore, the roguelike humor so prevalent in his other pieces. Historically, these satires are valuable for an insight of the public's view of an era; but, as literary works, except for some infrequent lines, they are singularly unimpressive for the most part to the modern reader.

I *William Pitt*

When George III suffered a brief period of insanity from October, 1788, to February, 1789, the question of the regency arose.[5] The Whigs (a term used here for convenience to discuss the opposition),[6]

believing they would be able to return to power, favored the Prince
of Wales. Pitt was in a delicate position; for, if the king recovered
and if Pitt had agreed with the Whigs, it might appear that he was
seeking to buttress his own political future. Pitt decided to seek a
limitation of the power of the regent, whoever should be chosen.[7]
Peter Pindar, who favored the Prince of Wales and his morganatic
wife Mrs. Fitzherbert, believed that Pitt would soon be out of
office because of the regency limitation which he saw as an example
of Pitt's own ambition for the throne since a regent would be
dependent on the prime minister. Peter Pindar, therefore, opens
A Poetical Epistle to a Falling Minister (February, 1789) with a
picture of England endangered by the youthful Pitt's plotting:

> Blind to an artful *Boy's* insidious wiles,
> Why rests the Genius of the Queen of Isles?
> Whilst Liberty in irons sounds th' alarm,
> Why hangs Suspense on Virtue's coward arm?
> Whilst Tyranny prepares her jails and thongs,
> Why sleeps the sword of Justice o'er our wrongs?   (ll. 1–6)

Turning directly to Pitt, the poet asks how the prime minister
could fix his fang upon the son, and bid Lord Rolle (1750–1842)
attack a beauty (Mrs. Fitzherbert). Speaking directly to the prime
minister, the poet says that he is "Dead to those charms that keep
the World alive" (1.52) and that he tries in vain to hide the prince's
virtues for his own benefit because he is fired with ambition "Like
Cromwell's, hot for power, to Thrones aspired" (1. 112). The poet
has been so aroused that Prudence bids him control his tongue.
Prudence states that, if the poet had more worldly wisdom, he would
praise the prime minister: "Strike to the *glorious* Pitt thy sounding
Lyre:/Thy Head may *then* be crown'd with Warton's Bays,/And
Mutton twirl with spirit at thy fire" (ll. 134–36). Pindar tells
Prudence that he cannot become a rogue or a sycophant, but she
replies that he'll then die like a beggar in a ditch. For once, to please
her, he will write as she wishes; and he pens the ode "On Messieurs
Pitt and Co." which, however, presents "King Pitt" (1. 5) as a vote
buyer who sends "to countries, borough towns, his Crimps/*Alias*
his vote-seducing Pimps,/To bribe the Mob with brandy, beer,
and song" (ll. 7–9). Prudence calls the entire poem ironic but
wonders when the world will become wise. This satiric ode concludes with a classical allusion ironic in intent and referring to

Pitt's ambitions; the Prince of Wales, in his own interest, should have played Bucephalus to Pitt's Alexander.

The king's recovery postponed the regency question, but Wolcot continued to mention Pitt in other works. The prime minister, the king's insanity, and the physicians' bill for treatment are referred to in *Subjects for Painters* (June, 1789). One suggested endeavor for the royal academicians is a painting of Pitt attempting to stop Britannica while she implores more money for the king so that he may pay his doctor's bills. "To a Nest of Lords" suggests that these gentlemen are all opportunists to whom friendship is only a word found in the dictionary. If Pitt were to be hanged, they would not rescue him if the next one in power gave them sixpence more in bribe money.

Pitt did not leave office, and the satirist was silent for a while about him. In fact, "To Mister Pitt," found in *The Rights of Kings* (1791), has very little to do with the man. In it, Peter says that power is very dear to a king; and he then wonders what punishment Pitt would prescribe for the academicians who failed to elect Thomas Laurance a member of the Royal Academy. No punishment is mentioned since the satirist claims the king wishes to be moderate after seeing that the throne of France could be lost for a song.

More Money! or Odes of Instruction to Mister Pitt (February, 1792) deals more with the king than with Pitt; for it is based on the rumor that Parliament is soon to be asked to increase the grant given the king. "Ode I" states that the request for money was invented by the opposition to discredit the king and the queen. "Ode II" instructs Pitt to remind George III that his unpretentious ways of living signify the king has enough money, and the remainder of the satire deals with the king's economies at home.

When Britain and France went to war in 1793, Peter Pindar occupied himself with references to Thomas Paine and to British political measures, hinting of the loss of personal liberty and of danger to the constitution. Pitt's measures to raise revenue through taxation of commodities never previously considered as a source for revenue, such as duties on "hats, ribbons, horses, linens, candles, calicoes, paper, bricks and even servants,"[8] brought forth a number of satires by Peter Pindar. On March 10, 1795, Pitt's tax on hair powder, besides becoming a subject for numerous songs and caricatures, led people to wear their hair as nature intended.[9] Peter Pindar's *Hair Powder; a Plaintive Epistle to Mr. Pitt* (June,

1795) deals with this means of raising revenue to combat France; and it opens with a reference to graft in high places since the money thus secured would "slake the golden thirst of Kings and Queens" (l. 2); those who believe in democratic principles would see the irrationality of using tax moneys to "Patch *ragged* crowns, and *cobble* crazy Thrones!" (l. 6). The nation, says Peter, is wearied of these numerous taxes and therefore damns the powder tax. Gray-haired oldsters who previously could produce an illusion of youth curse Pitt, and the poorest individual no longer dares to use ashes or flour on his hair. Hairdressers and barbers are not only pale but angry. Speaking for everyone, the satirist says the citizens want no more taxes; and, if Pitt should fall from office, no tears would be shed. He next intimates through animal imagery that Pitt may be in danger and that the example of America should serve as a warning to him:

> Mercy to England yield, the poor lean Cow;
> Thy busy fingers have forc'd milk enow;
> Though frequent rushing the lank teats to teaze,
> How patiently the Beast has borne thy squeeze!
> Just shaked her head, and wincing whisk'd her tail,
> When oft thou fill'dst a *puncheon* for a *pail*:
> But now she pushing roars, and makes a pudder,
> Afraid thy harden'd hands may steal her *udder*.
> Think on America, our Cow of *yore*,
> Which oft the hand with Job-like patience bore;
> Who, pinch'd, and yet denied a lock of hay,
> Kick'd the hard Milkman off, and march'd away.   (ll. 211–22)

Indeed, the next tax might be on human skin from which book covers and book binding could be made. Pindar then warns Pitt that his reputation is quickly crumbling because of his tax measures. If he taxes wigs and hair, the poet asks, how long will people be able to wear their heads?

On September 29, 1795, when the king was on his way to open Parliament, a mob cried out "No Pitt," "No War," "Bread"; and the king's carriage window was broken by a stone or a bullet.[10] Pitt and William Wyndham Grenville (1759–1834) had two legislative acts quickly passed to insure the king's and the country's safety. The Treasonable Practices Bill stated "that anybody who spoke or wrote against the Constitution, even though not following

either by an overt act, was subject to the penalties of treason";
and the Seditious Meetings Bill tried to limit gatherings of reform
societies by making it necessary for a license to be obtained from
local authorities for any meeting attended by over fifty persons and
"to have a magistrate present at such a meeting who had the power
to stop any speech, to arrest any speaker, and to disperse the
audience."[11] Although John Wolcot was not a member of any
reform society, he viewed the bill as an attack upon individual
liberty; he wrote *The Convention Bill* (December, 1795) to express
this opinion.

In "To The Reader," which precedes the poem, Peter Pindar
says that Pitt and Henry Dundas (1742–1811), treasurer of the
navy and one of Pitt's drinking companions, were not inebriated
when they had this bill passed. He ironically says that Prudence
who was there "presided over this Bill; which *wisely* orders that a
dozen Men, like a dozen bottles of Wine, shall not pass from house
to house without a permit." The "Ode to Mr. Pitt" finds that
Impudence, assuming Freedom's form, threatens to throw Pitt
from power. The poet then turns to details in the bill by asking
Pitt how many people will be allowed in a taproom since it appears
that "Sedition lurks within a Porter-mug;/*Eke* in a Glass of Gin
the knave lies snug" (ll. 25–26). Newspapers may be hotbeds of
treason; and rebellion may lurk in a whisper, a wink, a shrug,
in lifted eyes, or in a groan. No one will be allowed to mention the
king's name except the poet laureate. Peter Pindar wonders if men
will be forced to bed by a curfew; and, if a head peeps out a window
at night, will a bullet or a saber cut it down? The people should
submit Britain to the ministers and, like children, go to the school
run by "Goody Pitt". A voice, however, tells the poet that Britains
dare to speak and complain, and he who curbs free speech shall
be torn to bits.

When Pitt became a member of the House of Commons in 1781,
his first speech was in favor of economic and parliamentary reform;
but his precarious position as a youthful, inexperienced prime
minister and later the conditions at home during the wars with
France led him to hedge on reform policies.[12] Thus, any reference
which the satirist might make to Pitt as a reformer can only be
considered as an ironic thrust. In "Mr. Pitt's Flight to Wimbledon,"
which is attached to *The Royal Tour* (November, 1795), a reference
is made to the fact that a stone had been thrown at the prime

minister which caused him to flee to his country estate.[13] In this poem, Peter Pindar stresses the mob's anger and warns Pitt he may have to seek asylum in a hayloft or in Cloacina's seat. He advises Pitt to confess that ambition led him astray and that, when he spoke of reform, he never meant to keep his word. Pitt is like the country boy who slowly rose to become a grocer and then disdained any possession which reminded him of his former humble life.

Liberty's Last Squeak (1795) deals with the government's measures to combat sedition and treason, measures dangerous to literature:

> Farewell, O my Pen and my Tongue!
>   To part with such *friends* I am loath;
> But Pitt, in *majorities* strong,
>   Voweth horrible vengence on both.　　　　　(ll. 1–4)

Peter lists his former topics and subjects for satire; but now, since the reign of ridicule is ended, follies go free "Since Satire's a damnable Sin,/And a sin to be *virtuous* and *wise*" (ll. 23–24). The poet then becomes rather vicious in describing Pitt's and Dundas's drinking:

> No more must ye laugh at an Ass;
>   No more run on Topers a rig;
> Since Pitt gets as drunk as Dundas,
>   And Dundas gets as drunk as a pig.　　　　(ll. 37–40)

The other poems attached to this satire, treated in Chapter 6, speak of the loss of liberty when free speech is denied; and they depict informers busily searching for those who seem to be speaking sedition.

In *One Thousand Seven Hundred and Ninety-Six* (1796), the satirist, using a metaphor from botany, states that Pitt is deep in corruption; his roots are blighted though the trunk appears firm. "Tom" says that, when he becomes a writer, "I'll pierce of Wimbledon the midnight scene,/Where taxes spring, and Riot's orgies reign" (Part I, 111–12). Peter says it won't do any good; the king and queen will only smile. Later Peter tells "Tom" to give up the idea of becoming a satirist, for the prime minister will not allow any literature which hints of treason: "Pitt claps his paws on something ev'ry day;/A *hiss* at Royalty, a poor old Play" (Part II, 43–44). The "old Play" Peter Pindar speaks of is Thomas Otway's

Venice Preserved whose performance was checked because it was seemingly applauded because of its sarcasm about the king.[14]

"Tom" wonders just who this Pitt is who has stripped a nation, put liberty in rags, and brought England to the verge of destruction while the French are still successful in the war. Peter pretends that Pitt has some merit, but he reveals his disapproval of the war when he says, "Pitt fights our *just* and *necessary* war;/Improves our taxes (What would we have more?)/And sets an *honest spy* at every door" (Part II, 160–62). "Tom" says that Peter jokes about the ruin of the state caused by a man who frees informers from jail. The satire closes with the suggestion that there will soon be a dragoon at every door and that no reformation is in sight since the stupid public allows Pitt to remain in power:

> Pitt finds a tame old Hack in our *good* Nation;
> Safe through the dirt, and every dangerous road,
> The Beast *consents* to bear his galling load:
> And, spite of all that we can sing or say,
> Fools will be fools, and Ministers, betray.　　(Part II, 214–18)

In February, 1797, a run on the Bank of England made the government suspend cash payments and allow the bank to issue paper money; and there were more new taxes, including duties on tea, sugar, and spirits.[15] The result was restlessness on the part of the public over the conduct of the war; and on March 16, 1797, forty-three liverymen (guildsmen) of London sent King George III a petition requesting him to dismiss his ministers from his council as the quickest way to obtain peace.[16] Peter Pindar in his *Ode to the Livery of London* (1797) pretends to be shocked at the guild members' petition because it is impudent. The king and the queen won't be coerced into pushing Pitt out of office. Only impudence could have led them to inform their majesties that their minister lies and that he and pride are dovetailed.

Concluding the satire with "A Jermi-ad. Addressed to George Rose, Esq. of the Treasury" and referring to the Treasonable Practices Bill and to the Seditious Meetings Bill, Peter writes: "The birth of my *Jermi-ad* immediately succeeded Pitt's and Grenville's two celebrated Bills of Terror." As for George Rose (1744–1818), Pitt's friend who had left his position as secretary to the treasury when Pitt had left office in 1801, Peter finds him a man lacking in talent and of little education who "ascended by ladders of Impudence and Perseverance showing Merit and Modesty are not necessary for Fortune and Honours."[17] In the "Jermi-ad," Peter claims his power of satire has died to a whisper, for Pitt has cursed the Bard, a reference to the treason and sedition bills. This charge is most clearly expressed in concluding lines in which Peter says he must now shoot at smaller game since Pitt and Grenville agree "That Peter shall not laugh at Queens and Kings,/Permit me, *gentle* George, to laugh at *Thee*" (ll. 43–44).

On March 14, 1801 William Pitt resigned from office because of difficulties concerning Catholic emancipation which he had favored but which the king had not.[18] This event led the satirist to preen himself in *Out at Last, or the Fallen Minister* (1801). Peter's "Proemium" states that he had once said that Pitt would be out of office, but the man had acted like a wounded crow which took a long time to fall from its nest. Though some foolish people might want to try Pitt again as minister, Peter points out it isn't necessary since Pitt's tools are still in office. "Ode of Triumph" exclaims that the bull which tossed the Englishman is now impounded and no song of sorrow can be heard. In fact, England's Genius sings that the man who devoured the habeas corpus has been harpooned. "Poeta Loquitur" directly addresses Pitt to tell him that he had said he would destroy poets but he must now pay for his own coach. Pitt is now alone—except for his boundless pride which had never forsaken him. The newspapers will not attack him because of the tax on paper, and his red nose will lose its fire since poverty will not allow him his claret. Now that the gag is removed from his mouth, Peter will tell tales of kings and queens.

In the "Prologue" to *Odes to the Ins and Outs* (1801) which deals partly with the new administration under Henry Addington (1757–1844), the poet expresses his hatred of courtiers and vows to write his thoughts despite any penalties and pains it may bring him. He immediately follows with "Ode II. To the King. Written Immediately on Mr. Pitt's Retreat from Administration" in which the former prime minister is referred to with a number of homely metaphors of satiric intent. Peter says that he and everyone else is glad that the Jonas has been thrown overboard. Pitt was a bad steward who left no food, not even a mouse for the cooking pot; and, though he thought of himself as an eagle, the farmers thought him a bat or a kite. Liberty will now return to England, and once more the king is popular with the people.

"Ode III. to Lord Hawkesbury" states that this new foreign secretary thinks he is a man-of-war, but he really is a cockleshell. Peter suggests that the man should have asked Wisdom for wings before attempting this flight into high office. "Ode IV" again informs Prime Minister Addington that he is unfit for office and that it will be difficult to raise money: the udder of the state cow has been sucked dry by Pitt's followers. Warning Addington not to become a tool of Pitt, Pindar illustrates the danger with the tale of "The Monkey and the Cat." Seeing some chestnuts in the fireplace, the monkey uses the cat's paws to take them from the fire, thereby causing the cat to loose her claws.

"Ode V" is addressed to George Rose, who was formerly in the treasury under Pitt. Peter finds that this man is like the hedgehog who eats some apples but hides others in a hole; for Rose has retired to Scotland with pickings from the treasury. On the day Pitt left office, implies "Ode VI," the activities of Pitt's followers were like a mob's at a burning house "Where *friends*, amid the conflagration,/ With a *kind* thief-acceleration,/Whip off the goods they guarded by *desire*" (ll. 14–16). To Pindar, Justice at the time was bound and gagged; and her scales were missing. Stressing distaste for greedy officeholders unconcerned with the people's welfare, he discovers that the guardians of the state are "Just like a shoal of Sharks who swam in,/With Maws as wide as the Park-gate,/To *save* (by *eating* us) from *famine*" (ll. 42–44).

"Ode VII" claims that many people believed there wasn't anything which Pitt could not do, an example of how credulity blinds weak people. Illustrating credulity with "The Doctors: A Tale," Peter writes that a country bumpkin who lost his mule went to a quack doctor and asked if the quack's pills would help him locate his animal. The doctor assures him they will, the man takes a pill, and his bowels are soon on fire. Seeking privacy in a grove, the bumpkin finds his mule; and the village soon claims the doctor's pill is good for the blind, for the lame, and for finding lost cattle. Using a medical analogy, the satirist applies the tale to Pitt: Pitt was a cathartic which made the nation ill by producing an evacuation when it really needed a restorative called pounds. Pindar then relates a fable called "The Hedge-hogs" in which Squire Hedge-hog buries his money and tells council messengers that he is too poor to pay taxes. The messengers, after observing his humble home, agree; but, opening a newly raised hillock, they discover the treasure.

Squire Hedge-hog laments his crime and sorrow, but the messengers inform him that treasure in the ground belongs to the king. Peter applies this fable to Pitt by expressing the idea that the former minister, in avoiding his duties, placed the nation on an insubstantial foundation. Pitt, like a rat who dined in a house, undermined it by his burrowings; and then, after the plundering was complete, he left it to the fire and the rain.

"Ode VIII" says that Pitt, believing the country would fall without him, expected the king to ask him to return to office. "Ode IX" pictures the former minister as an alchemist who sent the finer parts of the state off into the air as he worked over the squires and the Bank of England in his crucible. When Pitt began the war with France, he thought it would be a fox chase or like a chase for a cat; but the cat, who turned into a bear, gave him a deadly hug. Turning to Pitt's friend Henry Dundas in "Ode X," Pindar tells him that, when the ship of state was floundering, something else was needed besides eating and drinking. Peter expects to see Dundas advertise for a place as butler, inserting the provision that he would not, if hired, be responsible for the theft of plates. If recommendations are needed, he directs enquirers be sent to him at the sign of The Bottle and the Glass. The satire closes with "A Moral Conclusion" which expresses the opinion that all which has gone before, political maneuvering, is a condition of the world resolved only by death.

II *Other Politicians*

Henry Addington, who became prime minister on March 14, 1801, and who held that office until May 7, 1804,[19] was never a major subject for Wolcot's attacks on politicians. Addington, rather, was used as a means to examine obliquely William Pitt; and events during Addington's administration allowed Peter Pindar to do so. *The Horrors of Bribery; A Penitential Epistle from Philip Hamlin, Tinman, to the Right Honourable Henry Addington, Prime Minister* (1802) is a two-hundred-thirty-line poem whose "Postscript" has been discussed in connection with the *British Critic*. This satire is based on Hamlin's attempt to secure the post of landing surveyor of Plymouth through bribery; he offered Addington two thousand pounds, was imprisoned, tried, and, on November 30, 1802, fined one hundred pounds and sentenced to three months in Marshalsea prison.[20] Wolcot's verse epistle, supposedly written by the imprisoned Hamlin who is awaiting sentencing, presents a man who protests his innocence because he believed he had been following political custom. Hamlin claims he didn't think he was doing any harm; he thought folks were bribed in London as they were in the country. At Plymouth great folks sometimes gave him eight or ten guineas for his vote; if his betters could do this, Hamlin felt it would be no wickedness to do likewise. His landlord told him the road to wealth was plain and that he should offer the bait to the prime minister. So he wrote and offered two thousand pounds, a procedure he "thort it was the *way* of all the land" (l. 132). The landlord told him to write to the minister's servants, but he forgot and wrote to the master. If he were released from jail, he would be ashamed to stir from his house; people and boys would point him out to jeer at. Hamlin pleads to know the verdict; if he is to be hanged, he wants to make his peace with God. Peter Pindar then, in his own voice, asks Addington to forgive the man and to allow him to go back to his shop.

The prose "Postscript" states that Judge Grose handed down a hundred-pound fine and a three-month jail sentence after stating that a minister's acceptance of a bribe for an office where merit alone should prevail would be a breach of trust. Peter Pindar agrees that a prime minister should be above accepting a bribe and that merit alone should be rewarded; but, if the judge had observed the political world, he would have discovered that few appointments and honors are made "on the basis of such an *unfashionable* and *solitary* claim as *merit*."[21] The judge must not judge the world by his own heart. In fact, the satirist believes "the learned Judge is, in *politics*, more of a *simple* Parson Adams than an artful and unprincipled Machiavel."[22] The reference to the character from Fielding's novel *Joseph Andrews* points out the discrepancy between the real world and the actual world, between viewing the world benevolently or realistically. Peter, by presenting himself as a realist, has thus emphasized the evils of politics; and, by pretending to accept bribery as a way of life, he has illustrated how common and with what unconcern the general public has come to regard such an action.

In *The Middlesex Election* (1802)—composed of six letters to Lord John Rolle (1750–1842), a friend of Pitt's in the House of Lords—"Joseph Budge," the fictitious author, states in Letter I that since Pitt has lost his place, he appears to be quite mellow. Budge tells Rolle that Sir Francis Burdett (1770–1844), a parliamentary reformer, will win the Middlesex election. Letters II and III deal with the conduct of the election, but Budge says in Letter IV that he believes that, when Pitt left office, he took all the riches that he could; and, while Grenville shared in the spoils, Canning received only a few tidbits. Letter V states that Burdett won the election, and Letter VI describes a visit to Pitt's home where the servant would not admit Budge because his master would not leave his port at the moment. Joseph Budge says that though Pitt rolls in guineas, the ex-minister will soon retire to Walmer Castle, live frugally, and pretend to be poor. The king won't take Pitt back again, but George Canning has suggested that a statue of Pitt be erected which would bring the man back into favor. Budge closes the letter and the satire with the thought that, if the statue is erected, a bust of the devil will be next.

   Pitt and His Statue (1802) deals, as the title implies, with the proposed subscription for Pitt's statue. In Peter Pindar's view, the proposal was advanced by the men who had loaned money to the nation and who had thereby picked the country of flesh through interest rates. Peter feels the statue cannot whitewash the former minister and says to those who advanced the idea,

> 'Tis very *kind* in ye, I'm sure;
> Yet 'tis but *rouge* on an old whore,
> That can't conceal the wrinkles and the scab:
> The Nation's eyes are vastly clear;
> Their scrutinizing power severe,
> Discerns a Vestal from a dirty Dab.   (ll. 9–14)

The satirist says that the proposed statue should be as huge as the Colossus of Rhodes and inscribed at the base with such words as "Reform," "War," "Old Bailey," "Income-tax," and "Penny-post" —thrusts at Pitt's legislative measures. The men who want a statue erected are told they make too much of Pitt; after all, a goose is not a swan. Lord Belgrave, who offered the motion in Parliament that the country should give a vote of thanks for Pitt's services to the country, is certainly an example of error; he thought a humming-bird to be an eagle. Well, a goose may think himself a swan—or a monkey, a man; and, if Lord Belgrave thinks Peter is joking, he need only look in the mirror. Peter claims he is not spiteful; he just wishes to save Lord Belgrave from folly and therefore advises him to be silent.

In the same satire, Pindar claims in "Proh Impudentiam! An Ode" that Pitt only pretended to love his country and that he had made politics a game which he lost. Who will pay for the costs of the game, Peter asks, which implies that the taxpayer will do so. Pitt was like a gambler who played for high stakes without having any money, or like the father who told his son, who is going into trade, not to become bankrupt for a trifle; for, if one goes into debt, one should do so on a grand scale. "Temporar Mutantur. An Ode" claims that the human herd is fond of power because it is stuffed with pride. Pitt seemed easy to control before he came into office, but afterward nothing could withstand him. In prose, Peter adds, "When Pitt is the subject I scarcely know when to remit the lash; he is such a feast for Satire."[23] A kingdom's calamities are often due to the ignorance of a minister, and the satirist hopes the calamity wrought by Pitt was not the result of malignity and vengeance.

III   Pitt Again

When Addington resigned his office, William Pitt again became prime minister on May 10, 1804; and he held that office until his death on January 22, 1806.[24] Peter Pindar believed Pitt would never return to office once he had left and his comments on Pitt now are muted and occasional. The prose introduction entitled "To Mr. Pitt" which opens *Great Cry and Little Wool* (1804), a series of seven epistles "by Toby Scout, Esquire, A Member of the Opposition" to his cousin Nicholas, deals with the dangers facing writers: "The numerous and too successful attempts of Ministers, and their Hirelings, towards the annihilation of Literary Genius, render it a hazardous undertaking for an Author to commit a liberal sentiment to paper. The mousing Owls of Power have so often hawked at the Eagle, that they have nearly killed it." Toby Scout wishes more freedom were available for others, and he reminds Pitt of something which he may have wished forgotten: "You, sir, have been an *author*; witness your various pamphlets on the *beauty* and *necessity* of a Constitutional Reform, printed in St. Martin's Lane; and which you endeavoured, by the most indefatigable industry to *suppress*, as soon as you arrived at the summit of your *modest* ambition."

Epistles I to III refer to the king's illness, and Epistle IV deals with the mother of George Canning (Pitt had recently appointed Canning treasurer of the navy). Meeting this woman in a park, Toby Scout records her rambling conversation. She no longer sells ointment, for she has an appointment from Pitt; and they will get a statue for him. Her son George has become a lord, her daughters will be courted, and her other sons achieve rank. Now that she is free from financial difficulties, she will be able to settle the nation's affairs. Toby's comment on this conversation, given in Epistle V, is to tell his cousin Nicholas that, if he should wish to receive smiles from the court, he should woo a petticoat. Epistle VI continues in this vein, but then speaks of Pitt's activities in the country: Toby claims Pitt is engaged in country sports and kills such animals as the sow, the calf, and the cow. In the evenings, Pitt sings a duet with General Moore called "Invitation to Buonaparte," whose lyrics invite Napoleon to England where he will receive a bullet and a pike for dinner and lodgings in a tower.

Epistle VII, the concluding one of *Great Cry and Little Wool,* records a conversation Toby Scout heard at his club: Mister Sly has said that the man needed for prime minister is William Pitt, a man who would give his last shirt for the realm, who had retired from his former office as poor as Job, and who is a moral person never seen in Venus's school. Dickey Dry replies that Sly gives a neat oration, but that it must be in jest. Under Pitt, continues Mr. Dry, if one opened his mouth to complain, the jail would open to receive him. That Pitt flees from the ladies should lead to its opposite proposition: do the ladies flee from Pitt? If Fame ever mentioned one good act Pitt performed, it must have been whispered. If Pitt had been sent from the heavens, the world would exclaim that the sky was passing off counterfeit coin.

Peter Pindar's *An Instructive Epistle to John Perring, Esquire, Lord Mayor of London: on the Proposal of an Address of Thanks to the Right Honourable Henry Addington, for his Great and Upright Conduct when Prime Minister* (1804) is a quite minor piece. Peter pens the ninety-six lines of his "Address to the Right Honourable Henry Addington" because he fears the address of thanks to this worthy man will not be signed. He hopes that the men who replace Addington will not be intriguers like Pitt and his minions whom he hates. If the king would only "Make *all* the motley pack *turn out,*/I'd seek Saint Paul's, and sing *Te Deum*" (ll. 29–30).

An "Elegy,"[25] one found in *Tristia* (1805) and one which must
have been written before Pitt's death, states that mortals are fond
of the marvelous. Drake, a painter, saw Pitt as an angel in the
skies or as a meteor. In actuality, Peter observes, Pitt made the
nation a workhorse through his tax program; and he proclaims
that he will continue to attack the man with "Willippics." Another
"Elegy,"[26] in this same collection of miscellaneous pieces, offers
an incorrect view of the cause of the minister's death when the poet
speaks of his own poverty which makes such a pleasant form of
"suicide" impossible:

> While others sink in seas of *rosy* Wine,
> Where *rosy* Pitt resign'd his boozing breath;
> No drowning oceans of the grape are mine;
> I *can't afford* to put myself to *death*.   (ll. 1–4)

CHAPTER 8

His Majesty, George III

SINCE the preceding chapters have briefly indicated that many of John Wolcot's satires dealt with George III, this chapter and the following one consider Peter Pindar's mode of attack and his opinions of the monarch; but a few biographical details of this king's life are necessary since the satirist was not only being factual but was also, in a manner, following what was almost a tradition—ridicule of George III. As will be seen, caricature artists mocked and lampooned George III numerous times, and Wolcot followed their lead with verse caricatures in which he recorded known facts and anecdotes about the king's person and activities.

By disregarding the public image of the man who wished to rule, guide, and control his country according to his own beliefs concerning the position of the monarch and who, in the process, lost the American colonies, one discovers that George III (1738–1820) was privately a pious and economically minded individual.[1] On October 26, 1760, two days after the death of George II, his grandfather, he was proclaimed George III, and one of his first public acts was a pamphlet issued on October 31, 1760, "against vice and immorality."[2] He married the homely Princess Charlotte Sophia of Mecklenburgh Strelitz on September 8, 1761; and she, from 1762 to 1783, became the mother of nine sons and six daughters. Both George and his Queen Charlotte practiced small economies in life, and both suffered from the roller-coaster ride of public approval with its up, down, up, down ride.

George III suffered periodic lapses into insanity which finally led to a complete breakdown in 1810 and to the appointment of his son as regent on January 11, 1811.[3] Peter Pindar did not deal with George III the insane person but with the friendly, economical king and with certain idiosyncrasies of the monarch. George III, who spoke quite loudly, jumped from one topic to another; and his voice was a "rapid stacatto."[4] Robert Huish, an early biographer, attempts to lessen this strange mannerism by picturing the king as a seeker after wisdom: "His majesty's method of acquiring knowledge was unique; it consisted of a system to which he inflexibly adhered of asking questions, and he would often ask three or four together, without waiting for an answer to either of them." Manfred S. Guttmacher, however, claims that "such speech abnormalities are associated with feelings of social insecurity."[6]

George III lived the life of a squire, for he was interested in agriculture and in animal husbandry. "He had converted large sections of Richmond Park and of the Great Park at Windsor into farm land—he loved to see land that was producing, that was doing its job."[7] Not only did he like to see land in use, but he also wanted to see it pay its way, for "he sent his produce regularly to market."[8] The result of this activity earned the king the nickname "Farmer George." "It was said that the royal pair were so greedy in the acquisition of money, that they condescended to make a profit by farming; and the royal farmer and his wife figured about rather extensively in prints and songs. In these the royal pair were represented as haggling with their tradesmen, and cheapening their merchandise. Pictures represent them as visiting the shops at Windsor, to make their bargains in person."[9]

Leading a simple life and dressed most of the time in his old clothes, George III would, while walking or hunting, "stop in some isolated peasant hut to talk volubly with its inhabitants and even taste the contents of the cooking pots."[10] Once he even helped to push a cart out of the mud.[11] Besides his economies in dress and at home, George III attended to his expenditures as a public figure: "Out of an income of more than a million pounds, he gave away only fourteen thousand pounds annually to charity."[12] George III was, as might be expected from these facts, niggardly in respect to the arts; nor was his taste said to be of the highest quality.

Thomas Wright in his *Caricature History of the Georges* (1867) records the numerous amounts of ridicule and satire directed toward George III and his family. Among many examples that Wright mentions, "On the 28th of November, 1791, appeared a brace of prints, reflecting on the household economy of the palace. In the first the King is represented in very uncourtly dishabille, preparing for breakfast by toasting his own muffins; in the companion print, the Queen, in homely garb, although her pocket is overflowing with money, is frying sprats for supper" (461). Moreover, Wright's *A History of Caricature and Grotesque in Literature and Art* (1865) says, "Many caricatures against the undignified meanness of the royal household appeared during the years 1791 and 1792, when the king passed much of his time at his favourite watering-place, Weymouth; and there his domestic habits had become more and more an object of remark" (471). At times, Wright states, Thomas Gillray the caricaturist pictured George III's "awkward and undignified gait, as he was accustomed to shuffle along the esplanade at Weymough; sometimes in the familiar manner in which, in the course of his walks in the neighbourhood of his Windsor farm, he accosted the commonest labourers and cottagers, and overwhelmed them with a long repetition of trivial questions" (473).

As these examples indicate, Wolcot, as has been noted earlier, was partially following a trend. It is almost a tradition that one attacks those in power through satire and caricature because of the fear of the abuse of power inherent in those who rule over others. By attacking those in power, the fear of unreasonable rule is lessened; and the hope is that such attacks will cause the subject ridiculed to become aware of his faults and follies in order to rule wisely. This reform is, in part, Wolcot's intent; but, in comparison to the other caricaturists of the period, he was more gentlemanly in his attacks. Peter Pindar's written depictions of royal foolishness are not so harsh as the caricaturists' graphic portrayals, but he does use their methods.

Peter Pindar presents the picture of the foolish king who asks inane questions, who has poor taste in art, and who is privately, perhaps foolishly, economical. Yet the reader is asked to laugh, to be amused, and not to be horrified by a picture of a stupidly avaricious monarch. The king is made a human figure, thereby lessening the distance between the private citizen and the royal person; he becomes the prudent head of the household and the family man. Yet, because he is a public figure, he is stigmatized— Wolcot's purpose.

Because George III is a king and a ruler, he must be shown how the world regards his actions. Peter Pindar then becomes a satiric adviser who points out that many actions do not coincide with anyone's concept of royal dignity. Peter Pindar wants a king to act and to look like a king, a dignified individual; therefore, Peter wants the king to examine himself for the sake of self-reform. Kings should have a nobility and royal bearing about them; therefore, they should act less frugally and more stately. Casual conversations with citizens on a low social scale should lead to admiration of, not amusement at, the sovereign. Frugality and economy should be practiced by those who of necessity need such traits and not by an individual who has such wealth that such characteristics lead him to be associated with the figures of Greed and Avarice. More detrimental culturally is George III's disregard for the opinions of those knowledgeable in the fields of literature and art: George III supports artists he admires, but he has no taste.

Although intent to encourage these reforms is implied in the satires of Peter Pindar, Wolcot also wrote to earn a living. What sold well, he would write; what was current and new, he would comment upon. And in these intentions lies the source of the dichotomy within the pages of Peter Pindar's satires. He wrote for money, and he wrote to illustrate the follies and foibles of public characters; but, working between these two purposes, Wolcot, it appears, more frequently wrote for the money; and concentration on the money reflects his realistic outlook toward life.

Wolcot's verses directed to the Royal Academy, to writers, to publishers, or to public officials produced no noticeable change in folly. George III was human, but he must be reminded that he was also a king and that he should act like a king. The example could be given, the reality shown to the man, but reform could not be forced. Wolcot probably realized this and perhaps knew how the king would regard the verses. Robert Huish might be retailing information known to the satirist when he wrote that Wolcot's satires produced on the part of George III: "no other effect, than a smile of wonder, at the perverse ingenuity of the man" and occasional laughter.[13]

Bearing in mind the king's idiosyncrasies, his tastes, and his political abilities and views, the reader can discover that Peter Pindar's satires were based on fact and that items were only slightly exaggerated to emphasize a point. Though the satires are discussed in order of their appearance, *The Lousiad,* whose five cantos appeared over a ten-year period, 1785–95, is examined in the next chapter. *The Lousiad* is Wolcot's most elaborate and sustained piece of satire, and this fact, plus the author's belief that it was a mock-heroic poem of high quality, call for a separate examination from the other satires which had George III as the satiric victim.

In his earliest work, Peter Pindar only obliquely and briefly referred to George III, but he gradually made the monarch the prime target of his criticism. "Ode II" of the *Lyric Odes to the Royal Academicians* (1782), dealing with Benjamin West, slyly questions the king's taste in art by stating that West must have some merit since he is close to the throne. "Ode XIV" speaks of the necessity for the artist of catching the true likeness of a man. Thus, if George III's or Lord North's portraits were exhibited, he, Peter Pindar, would not condemn a true likeness, for he scorns "to pass unfair and cruel strictures,/By asking for the *graces,* or the *souls*" (ll. 33–34).

In "Ode I" of *More Lyric Odes to the Royal Academicians* (1783), the poet complains of the lack of support for his genius when the monarch could make him happy with some modest aid. He doesn't wish to marry a royal princess, become an archbishop, or even take the poet laureate's place; he only wants enough money to be able to eat. In "Ode VI" of the *Lyric Odes to the Royal Academicians for the Year 1785,* the poet wishes the royal family was as fond of poetry as of paintings. If the king could think of some glorious action in his life, the poet would gladly commemorate it; and, if Peter's muse received fifty pounds, the muse would become quite prolific. "Ode X," however, offers a note of caution when he speaks of painters who wish to be in the limelight; it is a post of danger since no one is exempt from scandal and contempt. Who knows, the satirist speculates, whether George III "(Said by his Courtiers to know *every thing*)/May not by *future times,* be call'd a fool?" (ll. 27–28).

The *Epistle to James Boswell* (1786) states that the king has enjoyed Boswell's *Journal of a Tour* and may reward the author: "Oh! since the Prince of Gossips read thy book,/To what high honours may not Bozzy look?" (ll. 145–46). The king may even ask Boswell to dedicate the life of Johnson to him and "Asks questions of thee, O thou lucky elf,/And *kindly* answers everyone himself" (ll. 151–52). Referring to the monarch's conversational abilities, Peter says the king is no miser of his knowledge; George III spews out whatever comes into his head, "Free as election beer" (1. 158).

The poems pertaining to the poet laureate have already been examined, but certain aspects of them should be mentioned because George III frequently invited singers and performers to his home, for he loved the stage, and he "several times sent for Mrs. Siddons to the Queen's house, to recite tragic passages before the royal family."[14] Gertrude Elizabeth Mara (1743–1833), a singer popular in London from 1784 to 1802, is also one of the performers whom Wolcot mentions in connection with the king. *Ode Upon Ode* (1787) presents George III as an economical man, but the treatment compels one to call the monarch "cheap." The satirist speaks of the royal couple's fondness for music, especially if it costs them nothing. Frequently, they invited Madame Mara to Windsor and to Kew, where,

> No cheering drop the Dame was ask'd to sip;
> No bread was offer'd to her quivering lip:
> Though faint, she was not suffer'd to sit down;
> Such was the *goodness, grandeur* of the Crown! (ll. 119–22)

Furthermore, the lady was not given a single penny for her performance, a treatment similar to that of the famed actress:

> Poor Mistress Siddons, *she* was order'd out
> To wait too upon Majesty, to *spout*;
> To read old Shakespeare's *As you like it* to 'em;
> And how to mind their stops and commas show 'em.
> She read: was told 'twas very, very fine;
> Excepting here and there a line,
>   To which the Royal wisdom did object;
> And which, in all the pride of emendation,
> And partly to *improve* her *reputation*,
>   His Majesty thought proper to correct. (ll. 147–56)

While Mrs. Siddons read, she stood the entire time because she was in the presence of royalty and, consequently, became quite fatigued, "Nor offer'd to her was one drop of beer,/Nor wine, nor chocolate, her heart to cheer" (ll. 165–66). When a little prince noticed that the actress was pale and commented that she should have a chair, the king and the queen left the room so she could sit down. When Sarah Siddons left the royal couple, she was as rich as when she had entered the palace. Peter Pindar, who believed people should act like human beings, later offers this comment:

> Kings *should be* never in the wrong:
>   They never *are*, some Wiseacres declare.
> Poh! such a speech may do for a Birth-day Song,
>   But makes *us* philosophic people *stare*. (ll. 757–60)

Looking at Thomas Wharton's actual ode for the king, the satirist embellishes certain of the poet laureate's lines, but he adds a factual note in describing the king's ignorance:

> Of sharp and prudent economic Kings,
> Who rams, and ewes, and lambs, and bullocks feed,
> And pigs of every sort of breed:
>
> Of Kings who pride themselves on fruitful sows;
> Who sell skim-milk, and keep a guard so stout
> To drive the Geese, the thievish rascals out,
> Tha, ev'ry morning used to *suck* the *Cows*:—   (ll. 923–30)

The reference to the geese pertains to George III's belief that his cows were not giving enough milk. He was told that it was probably because of the geese, meaning that they worried the cows; but George III assumed that the geese were drinking the cow's milk straight from its source.[15]

An Apologetic Postscript to Ode Upon Ode (1787) contains the famous story, "The Apple Dumplings and A King." When George visits a peasant's hut and finds an aged woman making apple dumplings, he is amazed and asks her how the apples got inside the dough. The satirist's actual view of the monarchy is also presented:

> Far from despising Kings, I like the breed,
> Provided *king-like* they behave:
> Kings are an instrument we need;
> Just as we Razors want, to shave;
> To keep the State's Face smooth; give it an air
> Like my Lord North's, so jolly, round, and fair.   (ll. 139–44)

Actually, Peter Pindar feels that he is doing a beneficial act in criticizing George III since the poet regards himself as "Soul-physician to the King" (1. 205); in addition, he doesn't even charge the king a fee.

Robert Huish, an early biographer of George III, is always ready to sugarcoat certain facts about his subject, but he also appears prompted by a love of truth since he frequently offers much information which conflicts with his muted praise. An example is Huish's discussion of George III's visit to Whitbread's brewery, a visit which formed the occasion for Wolcot's *Instructions to a Celebrated Laureat* (1787). According to Huish, "His majesty always testified particular anxiety to examine whatever was curious in mechanism or the arts, and having frequently heard of the extensive brewing establishment of Mr. Whitbread, he determined to visit it, and accordingly due notice was sent to the proprietor of the honour extended him."[16] So the king, the queen, three princesses, and some courtiers on May 26, 1787, arrived a quarter to ten in the morning at the brewery, were shown about, and the king asked many questions "but scarcely ever waiting for an answer."[17] In the great storeroom which contained three thousand barrels of beer, "the queen and the princesses were so much amused with the store cistern that they went into it, though the aperture was so small as scarcely to admit their entrance."[18] At the conclusion of the tour, Mr. Whitbread fed the touring party, and the king offered to knight the brewery master who declined the honor.

Instructions to a Celebrated Laureat (1787) presents the king truthfully but as undignified in manner during his visit to the brewery. The king pokes his nose here and there, asks inane questions rapidly, and offers the knighthood to Whitbread. The conclusion summarizes Wolcot's views of George III's meager abilities and accomplishments. Addressing Thomas Wharton, Peter Pindar says:

> But this I tell thee, Thomas, for a fact:
>   *Thy* Caesar *never* did an act
> *More* wise, *more* glorious in his life. —
>
> Now God preserve us all wonder-hunting Kings,
>   Whether at Windsor, Buckingham, or Kew-house;
> And may they *never* do *more foolish* things
>   Than visiting Sam Whitbread and his Brewhouse!   (ll. 396–402)

Probably due to the king's lapse into insanity in 1788, the poet laureate wrote only one poem, and Wolcot's *Brother Peter to Brother Tom* (1788) offered some topics upon which Warton could have written. He could have mentioned that George III asked people to obey the sabbath, which led to the stoppage of concert performances on Sunday:

> Thus did the royal mandate through the town,
> Knock nearly all the Sunday concerts down.
> Great act! ere long 'twill be a sin and shame
> For Cats to warble out an *amorous* flame:
> Dogs shall be whipped for *making love* on Sunday,
> Who very well may *put it off* to Monday.   (ll. 123–28)

Cooing pigeons will be imprisoned, and sparrows and wrens will be shot "For being barely *civil* to their Spouses" (1. 134).

Peter digresses to explain that he dislikes the king because the monarch loves Benjamin West's pictures and thus "his walls, with tasteless trumpery drest,/Rob a poor Sign-post of its dues" (ll. 267–68). The king mocks Reynolds and cannot abide Richard Wilson or Gainsborough. However, the satirist can admire the virtues the king does possess: he is not an idle man, and he also seeks information. At a stag hunt, if no news of the animal's whereabouts is soon available, the monarch visits hovels and counts hens and pigs. No man binds books as well as the king; his son, the Prince of Wales, however, actually reads books (Guttmacher says that George III had a large library "not so much because he loved books as because he loved collecting.")[19] Continuing in a sly vein, the satirist sarcastically applauds the king's knowledge:

> Fair Justice to the Monarch must allow
> Prodigious *science* in a Calf or Cow;
>   And *wisdom* in the article of Swine.
> What most *unusual* knowledge for a king!
> Because Pig wisdom is a thing
>   In which no Sovereign e'er weer known to *shine*.   (ll. 379–84)

The Prince of Wales has never shown an interest in this sort of pursuit, which must surely prove that the father outshines the son.

Peter's Pension (1788) finds Peter exclaiming that there is no truth to the rumor that he has sold himself to the king; the king is too poor to be able to offer him a pension. Besides, their religions differ: the king thinks it a sin to dance or to play a musical instrument on a Sunday; conscience told Peter he might as well play the fiddle as the fool. To give the lie to the charge that the poet has sold out, Peter tells a story about George III called "The Royal Sheep." Some time ago at Kew, some sheep died, destroyed perhaps by dogs. The king told his steward Robinson that the dogs weren't mad (rabid), and the man takes the sheep to market where they were sold cheaply. Thus, the king is seen as so avaricious that he is willing to sell possibly contaminated meat to his subjects. To further prove that he has not become a member of the king's party, Peter tells "The King and Parson Young," which is based on a true incident. On May 20, 1786, while on a stag hunt with the king, John Young, a priest nearly seventy years old, fell from his horse; the horse rolled over him; and the injuries which he suffered caused Young's death two hours later.[20] There is no evidence that the hunt was called off, but it is known that a stag was later caught and that the dogs destroyed it.[21] The poem dealing with the accident states that the king enjoys the sport of hunting, "For tearing farmers' hedges down, Hallooings,/Shouts, curses, oaths, and such like *pious* doings" (ll. 5–6). Meeting Young on Windsor Terrace, the king insisted the priest join the hunt. During the chase, all horses clear the hurdle except Young's, causing the parson to fall and break his neck. The king orders a page to take Young home and have him put to bed, and His Majesty resumes the hunt without giving the parson a second thought. With this story Peter reveals not only George III's lack of dignity and his observance of the Sabbath but also his indifference to his fellow man.

"Ode IV" of *The Rights of Kings* (1791) offers some advice to Royal Academy members which illustrates Wolcot's views of the dangers of flattery when directed toward a mediocre person. Peter Pindar suggests that, if the academicians wish to maintain their good standing, they should copy the manner at court; for,

> There Adulation, with her silver tongue,
> Sweeter than Philomela's sweetest song,
>   Says unto Majesty *such things!*
> Tells them that Caesar won not half *his* fame;
> That Alexander was a childish name,
>   Compar'd to *his*, the King of Kings! (ll. 21–26)

"An Apology for Kings," found in *The Remonstance* (1791), finds the poet admitting that he has breakfasted, dined, and supped on the king—as a result of the sale of his verse. He will not praise George III, and the world should not expect wise things from a monarch who often lurches toward ignorance. He adds a story in which the king admires a statue of Hercules but wants an apron put about it because the queen is approaching. This anecdote shows, says Peter, that kings have a sense of decency and that statues should wear sacks.

More Money (1792), directed to William Pitt, speaks of the rumor that Parliament is to be asked for a larger stipend for the king. Briefly stated, this satire informs the prime minister that the king needs no money since the monarch is privately so economical. The best piece in this satire is "The Royal Bullocks. A Consolatory and Pastoral Elegy." The king tried a scheme of feeding his cattle solely on horse chestnuts, and the satirist asks the cattle why they are not merry but groan so dismally. Perhaps they want the chestnuts roasted, stewed, or boiled. Peter never says that it is perhaps impossible for cattle to eat the chestnuts, but he simply and ironically concludes the poem by saying they must live by horse chestnuts or die. "The Progress of Admiration; or the Windsor Gardeners" states that, when the king first went to Windsor, the gardeners invited him to sample every fruit grown on the estate. After chewing his way through a tour of the gardens, His Majesty granted the gardeners the privilege of sending him produce. Eventually, the gardeners hid when the monarch visited because he ate too much, requested too much, and gave them nothing.

The last reference in *More Money* to George III is in "The Progress of Knowledge." a "certain potentate" often visited Eton College where he asked the head master stupid questions about Caesaro, such as whether or not that Roman ever visited a brewery. The schoolboys began to mimic his unique speech mannerisms; "Thus every little Rascal was a *king*" (1. 44). Learning of this mimicry, "To *schools,* the Monarch bade a long adieu;/Of Eton journeys gave th' idea o'er,/And, angry, never mention'd Caesar more!" (ll. 148–50).

The Tears of Saint Margaret (1792), a minor piece dealing with George III's cancellation of an oratorio at St. Margaret's Church, presents the king as being dictatorial. Again Wolcot added minor pieces to fill out a slim pamphlet, but far superior is "Ode III" of the *Odes to Kien Long, the Present Emperor of China* (1792) in which George III is indirectly attacked by references to the activities which the Chinese potentate does not engage in. Directly addressing Kien Long, the poet begins:

> Great King, thou never educatest Swine,
>   Nor takest Goslings under thy tuition:
> Nor boardest by the week thy neighbour's Kine,
>   Like Pharoah's, that is, in a lean condition.   (ll. 1–4)

Kien Long does not watch the dairymaid at her milking, fearful she might sip a drop of milk. Since the emperor's behavior reveals a lack of wisdom on his part, he should learn such economical gambits as inviting only a few people to dinner and then selling the guests the game bagged while hunting. In "Ode IV," which continues the economic advice, Kien Long is told to journey to England for instructions from a pair from whom Avarice intends to learn some lessons.

One of the minor pieces attached to increase the Kien Long pamphlet is based on a true incident. On January 21, 1790, the king was on his way to open Parliament when a man threw a stone at him.[22] This incident is referred to in "Epigram, on a Stone thrown at a *very great* Man, but which missed Him." The epigram, given in its entirety below, turns the incident into a joke by an oblique reference to the monarch's thick skull:

> Talk no more of the lucky escape of the *head*,
> From a flint so unluckily thrown;
> I think very different, with thousands indeed;
> 'Twas a lucky escape for the *stone*.

After the king recovered from his attack of insanity, he made a trip to Weymouth, a watering place in Dorsetshire, on June 25, 1789, to aid the recovery of his health.[23] Thereafter, he made numerous and annual trips to this place where he could live informally, and he even purchased a home there. This journey was eventually satirized by the poet but not until 1795. In the "Domestic Occurrences" section of the *Gentleman's Magazine* for August, 1795 (p. 699), the following notice was printed for Monday, August 25:

This morning a little before six, their Majesties and the six Princesses, in a train of three post-coaches and four, with the usual escort and attendents, set off from Windsor, to Glo'ster Lodge, Weymouth for the season. The first coach conveyed the King, Queen, Princesses Royal, and the Lady of the Bed-Chamber. In the second were the Princesses Augusta, Elizabeth, Mary, and their Ladies of the Bedchamber. In the third were the two younger Princesses, Sophia and Amelia; their Governess, and one of the Maids of Honor to the Queen. The morning was fine; and several persons of both sexes attended in the Castle-yard, to be present at the Royal Family's departure. The same afternoon, at five o'clock, the royal party reached Weymouth safely; where, heartily wishing them every possible pleasure, we shall leave them for the present, and detail their progress hereafter.

Whether John Wolcot was present to see the royal family leave is unknown, but he could follow them imaginatively.

The Royal Tour and Weymouth Amusements (November, 1795) opens with the departure of the coach from Windsor Castle, and the satirist depicts the furious pace of the horses. The gawking onlookers of the animal world are presented in great detail providing a concise but humorous vignette:

> Dogs bark, Pigs grunt, the flying Turkeys gobble;
> Fowls cackle; screaming Geese, with stretch'd wing, hobble;
> Dire death his horses' hoofs to Ducklings deal,
> And Goslings gasp beneath the burning wheel. (ll. 21–24)

The stop at an inn for breakfast is used to caricature the king's activities: "Jokes with the Waiter, witty with the Host;/Runs to the Garden with his morning *dues;*/Makes mouths at Cloacina's" (ll. 36–38); and the poet slyly hints at royal parsimony by having the monarch take some apples without paying for them. Arriving at Weymouth to the sound of pealing bells, the monarch leaves the carriage, walks upon the esplanade, and bargains with tradesmen. The mail coach brings him his provisions since Weymouth is so expensive, a two-edged reference to George's cheapness; for the provisions sent from Windsor are transported at government expense. George bargains and haggles with farmers for bullocks, hay, and swine. He examines the fisherman's catch, orders some fish sent to Gloster Lodge, and doesn't pay for them. A sailor on crutches appears, seeking alms to support his wife and nine children. The king advises him to buy a wooden leg, but the beggar cannot afford one. After the sailor explains he lost his leg fighting for his country, George says this is a common occurrence and that the man is lucky he wasn't killed. The king advises the cripple to go to his parish for aid and adds that since he carries no coins he cannot aid him.

The king and the queen stroll about the town, then return to their summer home where the king reads but learns nothing. Returning to the seashore, George enters the water up to his knees, and the wind blows his wig off. Peter Pindar closes with advice to James Pye, the poet laureate—advice which emphasizes the lack of royal dignity in the king:

> Once more then let me beg thee, lazy Pye,
> To follow Monarchs wheresoe'er they fly:
> When, from the lofty pinnacle of Thrones,
> They sink, to tread, with vulgar folks, the stones;
> To Weymouth waves, and sands, and shops repair;
> Dash country Joans with dread, and Bumpkins scare:

> In laugh, and hop, and skip, and jump, and jest,
> For ever triflling, and for ever blest.—
> How like the rustic Boy, the simple thing,
> Who only wish'd to be a mighty King
> (So meanly modest was his prayer to Fate),
> To *eat fat pork,* and *ride upon a gate!*   (ll. 347–58)

The minor poems attached to this satire suggest topics which the poet laureate could write upon. "Caesar and the Fog" deals with the king's inane conversation. On an early morning walk about his farm, the king asks a carpenter what is new and is told that a fog was on Hounslow Heath. George repeats this information so frequently that the carpenter vows never to report any information on a fog again. The queen's economic ways are attacked in "Ode to the Elephant, Just Arrived from Bengal, as a Present from the Nabob of Arcot to her Majesty." Peter claims the elephant made the journey to please in vain since it eats too much. It should have been a more practical present, like a jewel:

> Now hadst thou been a diamond (no bad *size*)
> Or Pearl, or Ruby, how the Royal eyes
>   Had idolized thee! *gloried* to behold!
> Rather *too bulky* for a *Broche,* I fear,
> Or pin, or pretty Pendant for the ear;
> But then, thou wouldst have been cut up and *sold.* (ll. 7–12)

If the elephant wishes to stay, it should remove its stomach, cut its throat, and attempt to live without eating.

Another minor poem is based on George III's response to the crop failures and high price of corn in 1795.[24] The "Domestic Occurrences" section of the *Gentleman's Magazine* (August, 1795, p. 699) for Saturday, July 25, contains the following pertinent information:

His Majesty, with a munificence worthy of his station, has erected a mill in Windsor Park, where he causes corn to be ground, and retailed to the poor at 5s. 4d. per bushel: he some weeks since instituted a careful enquiry in the towns of Windsor, Staines, Egham, and their neighborhoods, for such as were objects deserving of his bounty; to these tickets were given, which entitled them to flour gratis. Excess and fraud were, however, the consequences and it has been found expedient to attach the present price to what must still be considered a liberal donation, since his Majesty's agents, last week in Egham-Market, gave 15s. 6d. for the corn, which, when ground, was disposed of to the poor at 5s. 4d.

Erroneously, Peter Pindar in "Ode to the Mill, Erected in Windsor Park for grinding Corn at a Cheap Rate, for the Poor" suggests that the monarch still makes a profit. To Pindar, this mill is also a questionable charitable act when one considers that the queen is still bejeweled in the midst of poverty. After a footnote that states George III stopped this charitable endeavor for fear he too would become a pauper, Peter writes: "The children of Famine poured in *too plentifully* upon the Royal munificence; which very soon must have reduced his Majesty to the *same* most pitiable situation."

The Royal Visit to Exeter: A Poetical Epistle by John Ploughshare (1795), Peter Pindar's attempt to re-create the Devonshire dialect in verse, traces the king's activities and procession in that city. The gaping populace is best presented in the report of George III's visit to the abbey in Part II. John Ploughshare writes to his sister Nan:

> Vull az an Egg was all the Church,
> Vor Voakes were mad az Hares in March:
>   And sath it was damn quare,
> To see ould dames wey leathern chacks,
> Hoisted upon the fellows' backs;
>   A penny for a stare.   (ll. 13–18)

Part III reveals the king's niggardliness by having him promise the local hospital a gift on his next visit and by reporting that the queen's and the princesses' clothes, all told, were not worth more than thirty shillings. The postscript to this letter to Sister Nan minimizes the glory of seeing royalty when the brother tells her not to grieve because she had stayed at home:

> Theeze once I've made my zelf a vool;
> And now I feel my courage cool
>   For zeeing Royal things:
> And when my Bible next I rede,
> Zo leet I worship all the breed,
>   I'll *skep* the Book of *Kings*.   (ll. 103–8)

This work of 1795 concludes the major references to George III, except for the role the king plays in *The Lousiad,* discussed in the next chapter. Other, but minor, references to the king have been discussed in the chapters dealing with Thomas Paine and with William Pitt.

CHAPTER 9

The Lousiad

JOHN Wolcot's most ambitious satire, *The Lousiad* (1785–95), was based on a true incident which had occurred in the royal household. Briefly stated, the king found a louse on his dinner plate, and he ordered all the kitchen staff to have their heads shaved. Robert Huish states that a living insect was found on the king's plate and that the cooks, after being told they were to be shaved, sent a petition to the king protesting this command.[1] Even Dixon, the chief or master cook who possessed very little hair, objected; but the protest was futile since they were shaved, except for a John Baer who was released from service.[2] Huish relates some information which may reveal Wolcot's source for much of his material when he states that Peter Pindar "was in the habit of dining, occasionally, at a coffee-house in St. James's street, formerly kept by an old servant of the late queen, to which, probably, the cooks resorted."[3]

From whatever source the satirist gathered the information, he used it for his mock-heroic poem *The Lousiad* which appeared in five cantos over a ten-year period and which was illustrated by Thomas Rowlandson. Such diligence on Wolcot's part deserves a complete chapter and commentary, and it should be noted that, though the poet allowed his imagination to guide him, he did retain the basic facts of the incident. Furthermore, if imitation can be considered a form of flattery and an indication of success, the poem was successful. When the *Monthly Review* for August, 1787 (159), examined *The Mousiad* by Polly Pindar and in November, 1787 (410) and *The Fleaiad* by Paul Pindar, it found that both poems did not equal Peter Pindar's talents and abilities.

Since there is no need to discuss Peter Pindar's critical opinions of George III, which have been sufficiently examined in the preceding chapter, *The Lousiad* should be examined as literature. This 2,661 line mock-heroic poem is basically written in heroic couplets; line 43 of Canto V reads "When lo, the King" and does not rhyme with any lines. The episode of the shaving of the cooks is told primarily in narrative-verse paragraphs, and Peter Pindar follows mock-epic conventions in most instances. A minor and silly occurrence is

magnified beyond its importance and placed on a level with a cata-
clysmic event. An exalted personage, George III, is made a comic
figure through parody of his speech and through an imaginative
re-creation of his actions during the event. Epic similes are attempted,
but these are found usually in two-line, homely comparisons and not
in lengthy verse paragraphs. Usually abstractions are personified;
but Discord, Fame, Prudence, and Zephyr appear as messengers
or advisers; and only Zephyr's actions play a decided part in the
course of events.

The epic traditions are mocked directly and indirectly. For
instance, the opening lines in which the poet announces his subject
and the conclusion in which the louse is carried off into the heavens
and made a planet parody epic conventions. Though supernatural
intervention often saves the hero of the epic and the mock-epic,
Peter Pindar's conclusion may be a parody of the fate of Belinda's
lock in Alexander Pope's *Rape of the Lock;* in fact, Peter Pindar's
title might be considered a parody of Luis de Camoes's *The Lusiad*
(1572). With a more direct attack and in more direct terms, Peter
Pindar mocks the necessity for an invocation, for catalogues and
lists, for long digressions, and for a tremendous battle; and Homer
is reprimanded because he originated these conventions which are
now expected in an epic. *The Lousiad,* therefore, meets and fulfills
its promise of being a mock-heroic poem by utilizing epic devices
and traditions in order to mock and parody them, as well as the
incidents that occur within the poem.

Peter Pindar's verse narrative lacks the turns, the yokings, and
antithesis within the single line associated with the work of Alexander Pope. John Wolcot presents a story in a straightforward,
newspaperlike manner. Antithesis is only achieved in two-line
comparisons: not with less pleasure does a man view the morning
light on the day that he is to be hanged. Wolcot presents a series of
dramatic scenes in which either the king or the kitchen staff is
mocked. Geniality, however, prevails; and the moralizing is kept to
a minimum, though it is suited to the events and speeches in a scene.
The moralizing passages may be considered part of the digressions
which expand the satire, and they are often witty and enlarge upon
the ramifications of the act.

Basically, then, Wolcot, in simple language and without a com-
plicated sentence structure, has produced a clear presentation of a
true incident; but he has also allowed his imagination to play with

the events. Besides skillful creation of dialogue, scene setting, and overall structure, he maintained his true purpose: the depiction of the folly and ignoble actions of the representative and symbol of the nation. The poem is suitably successful, but it is inferior to Alexander Pope's *Rape of the Lock* in technical brilliance but above Samuel Butler's *Hudibras* in comprehensibility.

Of all Wolcot's works, *The Lousiad* cannot stand alone; for all of the author's previous satires, with their references to Boswell, Benjamin West, Joseph Banks, and other prominent figures play a part in its humor and comprehension. For example, of the portraits in the home of the Goddess Discord, there is one of Sir Joseph Banks and his boiled fleas; the meaning would be lost to those who had not read Wolcot's satire on the man. An annotated edition of *The Lousiad* is needed if a reader is to understand the satire completely; and such annotations would deal with the personalities of Wolcot's times since the meaning relies on the depiction of individuals who once lived and who are colored by the satirist's prejudices and piques. Even if the characters in the satire are regarded as types, with George III as a male Belinda, it is doubtful that the poem would exhibit more universality; it is geared too much to Wolcot's times.

As a satire or as a mock-heroic poem, *The Lousiad* is not a failure; but it is a failure when one considers its lack of readers in the present century, a situation reflecting Wolcot's present literary reputation. By writing of contemporary events and personalities, Wolcot doomed his own work to his own lifetime—a period in which readers discarded Pindar and read the works of Sir Walter Scott and Lord Byron; and, for this reason, only a knowledge of the history of his times and its personalities can bring John Wolcot a larger audience. By realizing the limitation he placed upon himself, one can accept and appreciate his works.

I *Canto I*

Canto I (September, 1785) of *The Lousiad* opens with a statement "To the Reader" which declares that the events in the poem are true. Of more interest is the statement which reveals Wolcot's readings or knowledge of mock epics in which he declares his poem to be superior to all such previous endeavors: "The ingenious Author, who ought to be allowed to know somewhat of the matter, hath been privately heard to declare, that, in *his* opinion, the Batracho-

myomachia of Homer, the Secchia Rapita of Tassoni, the Lutrin
of Boileau, the Dispensay of Garth, and the Rape of the Lock of
Pope, are not to be compared to it."[4] The opening lines immediately
parody the epic conventions by their statement of subject:

> The Louse I sing, who, from some head unknown,
> Yet born and educated near a Throne,
> Dropp'd down—(so will'd the dread decree of Fate!)
> With legs wide sprawling on the Monarch's plate:　　　(ll. 1–4)

Beginning *in medias res,* Peter Pindar offers a series of epic similes
to capture the monarch's amazement and facial expressions concerning the event:

> Paint, heavenly Muse, the look, the *very* look,
> That of the Sovereign's face possession took,
> When first he was the Louse, in solemn state,
> Grave as a Spaniard, march across the plate!
> Yet, could a Louse a British King surprise,
> And like a pair of Saucers stretch his eyes?
> The *little* tenant of a *mortal* head,
> Shake the great Ruler of Three Realms with dread?　　　(ll. 45–52)
> . . . .
> Not more aghast he look'd when, 'midst the course,
> He tumbled, in a stag-chase, from his horse,
> Where all the Nobles deem'd their Monarch dead;
> But *luckily* he pitch'd upon his *head.*　　　(ll. 73–76)

Not with more horror does he look than does a rural maid at losing
a lottery or than a beau does when his white vest is dirtied by a
chimney sweep.

The king finally regains his powers of speech, and his speech
pattern is parodied by the satirist:

> "How, how? what, what? what's that, what's that?" he cries,
> With rapid accent, and with staring eyes:
> "Look there, look there; what's got into my house?
> A Louse, God bless us! Louse, louse, louse, louse, louse." (ll. 175–78)

When the king asks each household page if the louse is his, he receives
negative answers and becomes too perturbed to complete his meal;
but "His wiser Queen, her gracious stomach studying,/ Stuck most
devoutly to the Beef and Pudding" (ll. 207–8). The king analyzes
the situation, declares the cooks responsible for the indignity he has
suffered, and says they will be shaved and will wear wigs. In the
kitchen, the news strikes the cooks with fear, and they think the

louse belongs to Madam Schwellenberg, the hated mistress of the
queen's robes. The kitchen staff decides to remain firm; and their
steadfastness, revealed through similes, attacks royal foibles.
Sooner would the prince quit his bottle, his mistress, or a friend, and
sooner would the king eat his dinner without saying grace than they
will submit to having their heads shaved. A yeoman's speech approaches treason in suggesting that monarchs are human beings as
well as fools:

> Ah, me! did people know what trifling things
> Compose those Idols of the Earth, called Kings.
> Those counterparts of that *important Fellow*,
> The children's wonder, Signor Punchinello;
> Who struts upon the Stage his hour away;
> His outside gold; his inside rage and hay;
> No more as God's Viceregents would they shine,
> Nor make the World cut throats for Right Divine.   (ll. 433–40)

Ceremony and pomp have so blinded the world that it cannot
perceive monarchs are only human and not all-knowing; "Birth,
Riches, are the Baals to whom we bow;/ Preferring, with a Soul
as black as Soot,/ A Rogue on horseback, to a Saint on foot" (ll.
478–80). Royalty and nobility are of less value to the world than
cooks:

> Let Dukes and Lords the World in wealth surpass;
> Yet many a Lion's skin conceals an Ass.
> Lo! this is one amongst my Golden Rules,
> To think the *greatest men* the *greatest fools*:
> . . . .
> Accept this truth from me, my Lads; the man
> Who first found out a Spit, or Frying-pan,
> Did ten times more towards the Public Good,
> Than all the tawdry Titles since the Flood:
> Titles, that Kings may grant to Asses, Mules;
> The scorn of Sages, and the boast of Fools.   (ll. 507–20)

Canto I concludes with the cook-major's suggestion that they
petition the king to forgive them and to forget about the louse. This
reasoning is humorous if one considers their previous protestations
of innocence. A list of the shaved cooks is given at the conclusion of
these 522 lines of Canto I; it also records that John Baer refused to
be shaved and was dismissed from service.[5]

II *Canto II*

Canto II (June, 1787) opens with a long digression directed to the muses who are accused of inspiring persons with mediocre talents to become writers and of making poor authors proud of their petty abilities and productions. Pindar then calls upon Apollo to aid him "To sing sublime the Monarch and the Louse" (l. 102), and he remembers that an invocation was omitted in Canto I. The poet, deciding to write one now, calls for aid from conscience, who prompts men to speak the truth: she is a "Fair Maid, to towns and Courts a stranger grown,/ And now to rural swains almost unknown" (ll. 131–32). Half-seriously, he calls upon Fame to commend this present work to reviews, magazines, and newspapers: "Thus shall my Epic strain for ever live:/ Thus shall my Book descend to distant times,/ And rapt Posterity resound my Rhymes" (ll. 208–10). The satirist returns to his poem and mocks the convention of the epic invocation before attacking Mistress Schwellenberg:

> With tiresome invoation having done,
> At length our glorious Epic may go on.—
> Lo! Madam Schwellenberg, inclin'd to *cram*,
> Was wondrous busy o'er a plate o' ham;
> A ham that once adorn'd a German pig,
> Rough as a Bear, and as a Jack-ass big;
> In woods of Westphaly by hunters smitten,
> And sent a present to the Queen of Britain.
>
> But ere we farther march, ye Muses, say
> Somewhat of Madam Schwellenberg, I pray.
> If ancient Poets mention but a Horse,
> We read his Genealogy of course: (ll. 225–36)

When this woman was born, no commotion shook the earth, bees did not hang upon her lips, and no cupids played about her cradle. In fact, only an old, black cat was there who joined her in squall and tried to kiss her. Bats did fly into the room and shrieked congratulations to signify that she was one of them. The poet, however, says he must return to the calamity and stop digressing.

When Madame Schwellenberg hears of the incident of the louse, she insists that the cooks be shaved, and the king agrees. George III solemnly observes that first the locks fall and then the louse; but his solemnity is mocked by comparing him to a greater being:

> He spoke; and, to confirm the dreadful doom,
> His head he shook, that shook the dining-room.
> Thus Jove of old, the dread, the Thund'ring God,
> Shook, when he swore, Olympus with his nod.   (ll. 337–80)

The poet returns to the kitchen where the cooks grumble, and Dixon declares that Madame Schwellenberg has more hairs on her chin than he has on his head. Their petition, which Peter Pindar declares is not too sublime for a cook, is produced and read to the group; and the reading allows the satirist to attack abuses of the church:

> Thus reads a Parish-clerk in church a Brief,
> That begs for burnt-out wretches kind relief:
> Relief, alas! that very rarely reaches
> The poor Petitioners, the ruin'd wretches;
> But (lost its way) unfortunately steers
> To fat Churchwardens and fat Overseers;
> Improves each dish, augments the punch and ale,
> And adds new spirit to the smutty tale.   (ll. 641–48)

The petition, which concludes the 774 lines of this canto, appeals to the English sense of justice and even threatens the king. The petition declares that the cooks' heads are their own and contain no lice, but the owner of the louse should lose his hair. His Majesty should bear in mind that the cooks guard his belly; and, if he pursues his present plan of action, they won't prepare his meals. Moreover, to triumph over cooks won't make him appear to be another Alexander the Great. And the petition concludes:

> Lo! on th' event the World impatient looks,
>   And thinks the joke is carried much too far:
> Then pray, Sir, listen to your faithful Cooks,
>   Nor in the Palace breed a Civil War:
> Loud roars our Band; and obstinate as Pigs,
> Cry, "Locks and Liberty, and damn the Wigs!"   (ll. 769–74)

III   *Canto III*

Instead of introducing the gods as pieces of epic machinery into the 305 lines of Canto III (April, 1791), the poet personifies abstractions:

> Night, like a Widow in her Weeds of woe,
> Had gravely walked for hours our World below:
> Hobgoblins, Spectres, in her train, and Cats;
> Owls round her hooting, mixed with shrieking Bats,
> Like wanton Cupids in th' Idalian grove,
> That flickering sport around the Queen of Love.
> Now, like our Quality, who darkling rise,
> Each Star had ope'd its fashionable eyes;
> Too proud to make appearance, too well bred,
> Til Sol, the *vulgar wretch*, had gone to bed.   (ll. 1–10)

The king is asleep with his wife beside him; for he and she are "Unlike the Pair of modern days, that weds,/ And, in *one* fortnight, bawls for different beds" (ll. 15–16). Morpheus, who has closed each princesses' eyes, is unhappy to see the charms of these unmarried women thrown away. He, Morpheus, visits many people and brings them pleasant dreams:

> Of ancient Damsels eased the lovesick pains,
> Brought back lost charms, and fill'd their laps with Swains;
> Gave placid Cuckoldom a constant Dame;
> To brainless authors, bread and cheese and fame;   (ll. 49–52)

Silence now walks the land bringing a hushed quality to the city of London; and the effect of Silence has some sociological interest:

> Lull'd was each street of London to repose,
> Save where it echoed to a Watchman's nose;
> Or where a Watchman, with ear-piercing Rattle,
> Rous'd his brave Brothers from each box to battle;
> To fall upon the Cynthias of the night,
> Sweet Nymphs! whose sole Profession is Delight.
> Thus the gaunt Wolves the tender Lambs pursue.
> And Hawks in blood of Doves their beaks imbrue: (ll. 75–82)

The stillness of the palace is broken only by the soft footsteps of men who sneak quietly to the doors of the maids of honor, and they are as quietly admitted as they came. Yes, all is still except for (a glance at royal frugality) a fly looking for food, a hungry cat hunting for lean mice, a gaunt dog dreaming of a mutton bone, and the sound of hearth crickets complaining of colds and rheumatism.

During this still hour, Fame flies to the mansion of the goddess of Discord, the lady who stirred Satan to rebel, who told Cain to murder his brother, and who creates minor havoc among earth's inhabitants. It is she who dictates the tastes of the king, another hit at George III's critical pretensions. Fame tells Discord of the incident of the louse; and she, disguised as Madam Schwellenberg, descends to earth to whisper in the king's ear that he must be firm and must have the cooks shaved. He must act like a king, advises the goddess; he must prove himself a king since America and John Wilkes have shamed the throne. Then Discord, changing her disguise to that of Madame Heggerdorn, another mistress of the royal robes, hurries to Dixon to tell this cook-major that he must remain firm; and she also points out that George III had been frightened by the Gordon riots, a reference to the several days of mob action in 1780 over a Roman Catholic relief measure.

Dixon rouses the other cooks, and they all await the fateful dawn. Their woe and anxiety is described in a series of similes: not with less glee does an old maid view her younger sister's wedding, not with less happiness does the man condemned to hang see the sun rise, and not with less pleasure does a writer see his work condemned by critics. Absentmindedly, the cook-major whistles and hums; and the satirist once again openly mocks the epic conventions:

> Sing, Muse (or, lo! our *canto* not complete,)
> What Air he humm'd, and whistled all so sweet.
> Homer of every thing minutely speaks,
> From Heaven's Ambrosia to camp's Beef-steaks;
> Then let us, Muse, adopt a march sublime,
> And try to rival Homer with our Rhime;... (ll. 489–94)

Ironically, Dixon unconsciously whistles "Lillibullero," an old song ridiculing the Irish Catholics, and "God Save the King"; and Peter closes with "But wherefore, God Almighty only knows" (l. 520).

IV *Canto IV*

No omen, begins Canto IV (December, 1792), marked the eventful day: no raven croaked, no horse neighed, no sheep ran wildly about, no lightning appeared, no owl hooted, no jackass brayed, and no comet signaled that an important event was to occur. The wives and the daughters of the cooks gather in the kitchen to urge their men to have courage, remain firm; but, when Billy Ramus, who shaves the king, enters to tell them they will be shaved, only a unanimous groan comes from the assembly. A woman shouts that her husband will not be shaved; and Secker, a former clerk of the kitchen, reprimands her sternly. Prudence whispers in Secker's ear that no fame is attached to kicking a woman and offers him advice which mocks George III's pursuits and intelligence:

> Strive to surpass great Kings in binding Books;
> Transcend great Kings in forcing stubborn Kine
> To breakfast on Horse-chestnuts, sup and dine;
> In educating Pigs, be thou as deep;
> And learn, like Kings, to feel the rumps of Sheep.
> Go, triumph at the market-towns with Wool:
> Go, breed for Lady-cows the bravest Bull;
> Tower o'er the sceptered *great* in fat of Lambs.
> And rise a rival in the breed of Rams. (ll. 104–12)

Joan states that her Tom will not be shaved and asserts that the cooks are treated brusquely and shabbily because they are poor:

> Any thing's good enough for humble folk:
> Shoved here and there, forsooth; call'd Dog and Bitch,
> (God bless us well!) because we are not rich.
> People will soon be beat about with sticks,
> Forsooth, because they han't a coach and six. (ll. 158–62)

Joan, who knows her husband was never "lousy," says the louse may belong to Secker, thereby leading Peter to produce a mock-moral reflection:

> Muse, let us pause a moment. Here we see
> A woman, certainly of low degree,
> Reviling *folk* of elevated station;
> Thus waging war with mild Subordination.
> Should sweet Subordination chance to die,
> Adieu to Kings and Courtier-men so high: (ll. 197–202)

Lack of subordination would mean that the queen would have to mend her own stockings, as well as wash and iron her own clothes—a sight as strange as a vulture and a bat coupling. During the hubbub, the king and his entourage—groom, page, barber, queen, princesses, and Madame Schwellenberg—suddenly appear, and the canto closes with the king's reason why the cooks must be shaved:

> Louse-louse! a nasty thing; a Louse I hate:
> No, no, I'll have no more upon my Plate.
> *One* is sufficient: yes, yes, quite a store—
> I'll have no more; no more, I'll have no more. (ll. 299–302)

V   *Canto V*

The vain pleas of the princess royal against having the cooks' heads shaved opens Canto V (November, 1795), the conclusion of the mock-heroic poem. She says the cooks will bless the king if he will not have them shaved:

> Such sounds, so sweet, that most divinely broke,
> As might have mollified the sturdy Oak,
> Were doom'd in vain on Royal ears to fall!
> Yet Music drove the Devil out of Saul!   (ll. 9–12)

When the king asserts that they will be shaved though she pleads until doomsday, and the princess withdraws in tears, the rebellious cooks and their families, knowing now that resistance is futile, appear beaten by the mere presence of royalty:

> Sing, heavenly Goddess, how the Cooks behaved,
> Who swore they'd all be damned ere they'd be shaved;
> Who penn'd to Majesty the bold petition,
> And daring fumed with rebel Opposition.
>
>   Cowed, cowed alas! The Lords of Saucepans feel;
> Each heart so valorous sunk into the Heel:
> And then, each threatening Amazonian Dame,
> Her spirit drooping, and extinct her flame;
> For lo! of Majesty the powerful Blaze,
> His Coat's bright Gold, and Eyeball's rolling Gaze,
> Just like the Light that covered sad Saint Paul,
> Flashed on their visages, and smote them all. —   (ll. 52–63)

This description of the king's ability to quell turmoil leads to a digression which indicates that the position of king is losing its magical powers. Homage to the throne has disappeared, and Lady France,

> Nay, dares to fancy (an old rebel jade)
> *Emperors* and *Thrones* of *like materials* made;
> Nay, fancy too (on bold Rebellion's brink,)
> That Subjects have a *right* to *speak* and *think*;
> Revileth Kings, for praise and wonder born;
> Calleth Crowns Fool's Caps, that *their* heads adorn;
> And Sacred Sceptres, which we *here adore*,
> Mean Picklocks for the houses of the poor.   (ll. 94–101)

Old gray-haired Dixon in one last plea that he be spared says, "Man should be kind to man, O Best of Kings,/ And try to blunt the ills that Nature brings" (ll. 120–2); but Madam Schwellenberg interrupts to call him a saucy fellow who beats the Methodists in preaching. The queen consoles him with the statement that wigs are in fashion; and, unaware of the shame attached to having one's head shaved, she exclaims, "Mine Gote! de tremblin fellow seem afred,/ As if we put a Tiger 'pon his head" (ll. 152–53). To her, the kitchen staff should be thankful that only their hair is being cut off.

The king says he will show mercy by paying for their wigs, but this impulsive bit of generosity is squelched by Avarice, a lean maiden,

> Who fiercely snatch'd, with wild devouring eyes,
> An atom of Brown Sugar from the Flies;
> Made a sad Candle from a dab of Fat,
> And stole a stinking Fish-head from a Cat;
> Saves of the mustiest Bread the Crumbs, and sees
> A Dinner in the *scrapings* of a Cheese: (ll. 178–83)

With marvelously ridiculous reasoning, Avarice tells George III that buying the cooks' wigs would encourage the breeding of lice; moreover, wigs cost a great deal of money. The great should be an example to the poor by living frugally, as does the queen, who can "Transform an old silk stocking into *mits*;/ Transform too (so convertible are things)/ E'en flannel petticoats to caps for Kings" (ll. 257–9). Avarice concludes her advice by telling George III not to buy the wigs since it is flinging good money away in wasted kindness; the king agrees.

The cooks are shaved; but the poet bemoans the fact that no battle took place since an epic poem demands one:

> How could I hold aloft my tuneful head,
> Or proudly hope at Doomsday to be read;
> The glowing wish of every Son of Rhyme,
> To live a favourite to the end of time?   (ll. 392–95)

A battle, however, is a simple thing to produce:

> Yet nought were easier than to raise a Battle;
> Make iron head-piece against head-piece rattle;
> Nails nails oppose, and grinders grinders greet,

> Nose poke at nose, and stomachs stomachs meet;
> Wild-rolling eye-balls against eye-balls glare;
> The dusty floor be strew'd with teeth and hair;   (ll. 398–403)

In any event, the king is happy, and he takes out the pill box in which the louse has been imprisoned. The louse, like Balaam's ass, is given the power of speech, and he tells his life story. Born, raised, and married to Lousilla in a page's locks, he and his wife fell on the hair of a dairymaid when she was wrestling with his former host. From her, the couple crawled to the untidy king:

> "Where, safe from nail and comb, and blustering wind,
> We nestled in your little Lock behind;
> Where many a beauteous Baby plainly proves,
> Heaven, like a King's, can bless a Louse's loves;   (ll. 446–49)

One day the louse decided to stray; and, as a result, he fell upon the king's dinner plate and his wife and the children—Nittilla, Grubbinetta, Snap, Diggory, Scratch, and little Nibble, the youngest—are in mourning. Therefore, the louse informs the king that his majesty is wrong in blaming the cooks. Crying out that this tale is a pack of lies, the king aims his fingernails at the louse, who, through Zephyr's aid, escapes and is transported to the heavens to become the planet Uranus which Sir William Herschel (1738–1822) discovered on March 13, 1781, and wished to honor George III by calling it the "Georgium Sidus."[6] Thus, the ludicrous event ends in ridicule to insure that the planet will remind his majesty of his folly:

> Yet to the Louse was *greater* glory given;
> To roll a Planet on the splendid Heaven,
> And draw of deep Astronomers the ken,
> The *Georgium Sidus* of the Sons of Men!!!   (ll. 504–7)

CHAPTER 10

Miscellaneous Satires

THE previous chapters discussed satires loosely united through the professions of the figures attacked, but some of Pindar's satires do not fit one particular category. These verses, based on political and social events, have no unifying theme; but the satirist's stance is evident when each is discussed. No summary will deal with them in general because Wolcot's views are primarily the same in every satire, and a summary would merely echo his previous statements. To avoid repetition, this discussion is limited, therefore, to satires which treat new subjects or ones not hitherto discussed.

I *The Bad Earl*

James Lowther, Earl of Lonsdale (1736–1802), who was instrumental in having William Pitt admitted into Parliament from his pocket borough of Appleby, Westmoreland, was a wealthy man as owner of the collieries of Whitehaven, Cumberland.[1] A detested tyrant of his tenants, Lowther "was known throughout Cumberland and Westmoreland as the 'bad earl.'"[2] "A Litigious disposition, or rather a determination to oppress, by means of wealth, and under colour of law, all who were obnoxious to him, has been frequently imputed to Lord Lonsdale; and the records of the courts, the books of reports, and the account of the assizes in different counties, have appeared, for a long series of years, to afford some basis for the imputation."[3]

The earl's activities in conjunction with the town of Whitehaven aroused Wolcot's disapproval and he wrote *A Commiserating Epistle to James Lowther, Earl of Lonsdale* (1791). This 318-line satire explains its *raison d'être* in the introduction, which consists of three letters. Because of mining activities in Whitehaven, a Mr. Littledale's home, plus other houses, collapsed; and, when Mr. Littledale sought reimbursement from the earl, he, angered at such presumption, closed the mines. When one hundred and thirty-five Whitehaven citizens wrote to the earl stating that the town would pay any court costs and the costs of future prosecutions if the earl would reopen the mine, the earl replied that every person must be responsible for his own property and that a new trial would soon contest Littledale's claims. The people wrote again to say they would accept responsibility for accidents on their own property if these were not connected with the mines.

These letters serve as an introduction to the poem, which attacks the earl for his coldness and cruelty. The verse epistle mockingly bids the earl not to "Yield to the anger of a tiny *town*,/ Who oft has frighten'd *countries* with a frown!" (ll. 5–6). If he merely thought of yielding, his ancestors would arise and shake him—a remark leading to commentary on the history of the Lowthers: "Look through the desert of five hundred years!/ Lo, not a Lowther virtue *once* appears" (ll. 15–16). If the earl did one virtuous act, the world would not believe it. Pindar tells Lowther to look at the oak tree beneath whose branches and trunk the ants are crawling, for a resemblance exists between the man and the oak. The earl, however, should spurn meekness and forgiveness and wrap himself in his pride; Whitehaven and all of Cumberland should feel his power as the earl becomes the canker in the rose.

Bidding the earl to expel pity, virtue, generosity, and other virtues from himself, Peter reveals that people desire power "To look contemptuous on the World below;/ To bid *that* World bow down, admire, adore;/ And grind the sallow faces of the Poor" (ll. 142–44). The earl should add to his fame by having a game law passed which permits him to hunt down farmers' wives and daughters. He should curse modern liberty and wish to hang the French dogs who turned on the huntsmen. If he wants to be adored and trembled at, he should keep the people poor, teach them a lesson, and horsewhip them: "Eye nature through, and mark the arm of Pow'r:—/ The great unceasingly the small devour" (ll. 233–34). The spider devours the trapped fly, and the kite swoops down on chickens in spite of the cries and capers of the hen or the curses of the farmer running for his gun. And James Lowther should emulate the spider, the kite, or the alligator, the whale, or the shark. Then, in lines of mock advice, Peter Pindar again comments on the man's lack of virtue:

> Lo, at thy foot, the People whine and pray:
> But kick them, Lonsdale; 'tis the *Lowther way*:
> Tread on each Neck, and deem it but a Beast,
> And emulate the Tyrants of the East.   (ll. 279–82)

The earl should not listen to Whitehaven's prayers, for the people despise him; after all, he did nothing to win approbation. Instead, he should be the kite over these sparrows; unmuzzle vengeance; bid goodbye to humanity; and wave the flag of tyranny over his walls. "Thus at thy feet shall dumb Obedience fall,/ And Hell in lustre yield to Lowther Hall" (ll. 317–18). These lines were quite libelous, and the earl did not suffer in silence: "In February 1792 he brought an action in the Privy Council against John Wolcot."[4] The case, however, was dropped.

II Chinese Overtures

In 1792, Britain wished to establish a more favorable trading position in China as well as to alleviate Chinese acts of injustice toward English merchants. On September 26, 1792, George Macartney (1737–1806), the colonial governor of Madras, India, from 1780 to 1786 and a member of the Irish House of Peers, set forth on the ship *Lion* as the plenipotentiary of the diplomatic mission.[5] Though he was treated with respect and though he himself avoided the Chinese style of homage, the kowtow to the emperor, Macartney was unsuccessful in establishing an ambassador in China, and he returned to England in September, 1794.[6] This mission to China led Wolcot to make a few witty remarks at George III's expense.

In *A Pair of Lyric Epistles to Lord Macartney and His Ship* (1792), published before Macartney's return, Pindar advises the ambassador, in "A Lyric Epistle to Lord Macartney," to tell Kien Long, the emperor of China, that subordination has died in England. He should also speak of the army exercises conducted by the duke of Richmond on Bagshot Heath, which is viewed as a show of force to make Thomas Paine hold his tongue. This first epistle has very little to do with the embassy, but the second epistle "To the Ship" is more pertinent and witty. Peter hopes the embassy will be successful, and then he imaginatively constructs the journey. In Canton, the natives and the mandarins will turn pale when they hear the salutation gun, and the trip to Peking will be filled with dubious honors:

> Pagodas of Nang-yang, and Chou-chin-chou,
> So lofty, to our traveling Britains bow;
>   Bow, Mountains sky-enwrapp'd of Chin-chung-chan;
> Floods of Ming-ho, your thundering voices raise;

> Cuckoos of Ming-fou-you, exalt their praise,
> With geese of Sou-chen-che, and Tank-ting-tan.
>
> O Monkeys of Tou-fou, pray line the road,
> Hang by your tails, and all the branches load;
> Then grin applause upon the gaudy Throng,
> And *drop* them *honours* as they pass along.   (ll. 13–22)

Pindar sees the coaches reach Peking and sees the emperor frown. When Kien Long will ask what the British want, Macartney will say to barter for diamonds or similar things. The emperor of China will have the visitors stripped and beaten with bamboo canes and foolscaps placed on their heads as the reward for their folly. If all this occurs as Peter imagined it, the vessel will not dare return to England; but, if the mission is successful, the greedy court will be pleased "to find as many Gems on board,/ As will not leave thee room to stick a pin!" (ll. 85–86).

Not willing to allow a fresh source of satire to die, Peter Pindar followed the Macartney poems with *Odes to Kien Long* (1792), which contains not only five poems addressed to the emperor of China and are satires against George III, but also thirteen other poems on various subjects, some previously mentioned in connection with other satires. The prose preface states Peter's hope that, since Macartney will open trade with China, a literary trade may occur between the emperor and the satirist. They are very much alike: rhymers, geniuses, lovers of novelty, and idolators of royalty. To prove he can pay for trade goods, he sends Kien Long specimens of his work.

"Ode I" says that, for a king, Kien Long writes some good rhymes. It pains him, though, to see some Western kings indifferent to poetry and interested only in farming:

> Kings deem, ah me! a grunting Herd of Swine
> Companions sweeter than the tuneful Nine:
> Preferring to Fame's Dome a Hog-sty's mire;
> The Roar of Oxen to Apollo's Lyre.   (ll. 29–32)

"Ode II" informs Kien Long that he is a second Atlas, for he supports half the world. Most thrones are so high that the kings cannot see their subjects, but a great change has been produced by France: now the public sees no merit in birth and believes virtues have left the palace. "Ode III" and "Ode IV" attack George III, and "Ode V" contains Peter's view of the embassy: England has heard tales of China's wealth and has sent a ship for trading purposes. Royalty wonders what the emperor has to give away, for it is rumored he is generous; but he should not expect the king and queen to send much in return. The king might send a farm animal and some fowls; the queen, a pound or two of snuff and a history of Strelitz, the place of her birth. Kien Long, however, should send heaps of things, even if George had to build barns to hold the goods; the emperor really cannot send too much. If he gave the entire Chinese Empire, Madam Schwellenberg, the queen's mistress of the robes, would only wonder if that were all. If Kien Long would cram the ship full, the people would say it was a good trip.

Macartney's unsuccessful mission produced "Ode to the Lion Ship of War, on her Return with the Embassy from China," one of the poems in *Pindariana* (1794). Peter welcomes back the ship whose ensign at half-mast produces laughter. The journey proved that Eastern monarchs were very proud, and at Kien Long's court the embassy received not one bit of applause. Avarice must have planned the expedition, and a fool must have told the king it would thrive; perhaps the fool said that, since India succumbed, China would do likewise. In this short satire, it is obvious that the satirist used the incident not only to attack George III but also to express obliquely his views on liberty and freedom.

III   *Legislated Morality*

Lord Auckland's Triumph (1800) deals with the intended passage of Auckland's proposed Criminal Conversation Bill, which would prevent adulterers and adultresses from remarrying. Only two odes are concerned with this proposal; the remainder of the pamphlet, three poems and a prose postscript, refers to the critical attacks on the satirist's poem *Nil Admirari*. Peter Pindar considers the Criminal Conversation Bill vindictive since adulterers could not marry; and, through mockery and irony, he pleads for common sense in this matter. "To Lord Auckland," the satire's prose preface, speaks of the loose morals of the period: "The increasing depravity of the Fair Sex cries aloud for correction; Adultery is deemed a Peccadillo, and Fornication a mere Flea-bite: gigantic are the strides that Lewdness has taken to subdue the moral world; her steps are like those of Neptune, from promontory to promontory." Every woman is now accomplished and handsome; and, at every turn, a Cleopatra can be met and obtained for a halfcrown. For the sake not only of great families but also of honor, the satirist hopes the bill will be successful; therefore, he dedicates his odes to Lord Auckland.

"Ode I" calls the song of wedded love sweet and asserts that only a ruffian would invade and turn it into a song of woe. Because of Auckland's bill, the lawless reign of adultery is over, and no husband need fear cuckold's horns. Ironically, Peter has mocked the bill by asserting that morality can be legislated, that all individuals obey the laws. Auckland is seen as wiser than the folks who lock stable doors after the horse is stolen. Peter then becomes autobiographical and presents his youthful attitude toward loose ladies:

> Blushing I own, I've been in love with Pleasure;
> Look'd on the Nymph's acquaintance as a treasure;
>   Never pursued her once with scoff and hisses:
> But caught the little Hussy in my arms;
> Ran o'er the pretty Garden of her Charms,
>   And pluck'd the Cherries of her lips, call'd Kisses.   (ll. 73–78)

Now he is more sober, but the times are more wicked since ladies no longer wear flannel petticoats, caps, or high-collared dresses. Such was not the case in the past when grandmothers were well bundled: "How different from our modern Fair,/ Whose every beauty *takes the air!*" (ll. 125–26). Well, King David and King Henry set bad examples for wedlock; but some princes are not wicked as the story of the king of France illustrates. In "A King of France and the Fair Lady at Battledore and Shuttlecock," the shuttlecock falls down the lady's bodice, and, when she asks the king to retrieve it, he does so with chimney tongs. Peter adds that, if British princes were asked to perform the task, they would retrieve it with their hands, and search the bosom all day if necessary.

"Ode II" deals with the effect the passage of a Criminal Conversation Bill would have upon the general public. Only a son of Satan would tell a woman that he hates constancy and doesn't wish love encumbered by marriage vows; so, since her husband is out of town, they should skip to the field where she will receive a green gown. Everyone says that, if Criminal Conversation dies, glory would return to the British Isles. Old age and eighteen-year-old virgins would no longer be seen together. The aged husband would no longer fear the horns, and the old rake would be pleased. Another rake says that he will still be able to bound all over his neighbor's ground, but his own wife will die at home because of the bill. Only the pimps, the writers of salacious and prurient tales, and the hawkers of transcripts of criminal-conversation trials will mourn if the bill is passed. With Adultery declared legally dead, her sister Miss Fornication will appear at masquerades, and Hypocrisy will now aid her. Peter concludes that morality cannot be legislated; therefore, criminal conversation need not fear Lord Auckland, who will still tremble at visionary horns.

The three poems attached to this satire pertain indirectly to passion. "Advice to Young Women; or, the Rose and Strawberry. A Fable" finds a rose in bloom asking the strawberry why it hides its charms. The strawberry says it lacks pride, is afraid, and is safer in the shade of her leaves. The rose calls her simple and points out that she, herself, wantons in the wind and the sun visits her charms. This admission is no sooner made than a country lad plucks the rose, smells her, and places her in his hat. No moral is given because the moral is obvious: beauty which displays herself is soon ravished.

In the "Ode to Hymen," the poet wonders why folks don't live in harmony and why passions ebb so quickly. Using a geographical metaphor, Peter Pindar traces the progress of love:

> Love seems at first within the *torrid* zone;
>   Now to the *temperate*, lo, his course he bends;
>   Now to the *frigid* limpeth with a groan,
>   And now the sweetest of all passions *ends*!   (ll. 9–12)

As an example of love's waning, Peter examines a country clown on his honeymoon. Lubin sweetly tells his bride to put her pretty little toes next to his; after the honeymoon, he tells her to heave her great hocks away from him.

In "Ode on the Passions," the satirist is in an autobiographical, playful, and advice-giving mood. In respect to women, men like to smell a flower or pluck and devour a peach; in other words, men like variety found out of wedlock. He, in his youth, kissed and pressed various charmers, but now he is by heaven's grace reformed and can offer advice:

> O Youths! where'er the wishes warm of Nature
>   Tumultuous rise, destroy their dangerous dance;
>   The curb of reason to your aid advance,
> And souse them with her buckets of cold water.   (ll. 27–30)

Using the candle as an example, Peter points out that there is no harm in the passions if they are properly controlled. The candle's flame is quiet and steady; but, if it touched the bed curtains, it could bring the house down.

IV *Bribery and Mrs. Clarke*

In 1808, Parliament investigated the army's patronage system due to the conduct and activities of Mrs. Mary Anne Clarke (1776-1852), mistress of Frederick, Duke of York, who, as commander-in-chief of the army, had a great deal of patronage to bestow. The duke irregularly paid his mistress one thousand pounds a month, her creditors pressed her, and she soon began taking money for her influence in securing army promotions and positions.[7] Although eight charges were brought against the Duke of York in 1809, nothing could be proved; but there was no doubt that Mrs. Clarke had received the bribes. The duke resigned his position and broke off his connection with his mistress; in retaliation, Mrs. Clarke decided to publish her former lover's letters, but she was bought off for seven thousand pounds and a pension of four hundred pounds a year.[8] At the trial itself, Mrs. Clarke came off handsomely since "her beauty and courage, and even the sauciness with which she stood her long continuation at the bar of the house, won her many admirers."[9] This *cause célèbre* did not pass unnoticed by Peter Pindar, who wrote *A Solemn, Sentimental and Reprobating Epistle to Mrs. Clarke* (1809) and then *A Second Epistle to Mrs. Clarke* (1809).

In the first epistle of 188 lines in heroic couplets, Peter says he "With deep *reluctance* now assumes the rod,/ To *punish* that fair Master-piece of God" (ll. 5–6). He finds this beauty is now the cause of dire confusion; every hotel, taproom, and coffeehouse speaks only of the Duke and Mistress Clarke and of the possible fall of the government. Although everything is in a hubbub, Pindar hopes the goddess of Delicacy will come to mend everyone's manners; the goddess should "A Gothic race to some refinement raise;/ For even our Quality have *dirty* ways" (ll. 111–12). But should the mob tell the Lord's viceregents what to do? How should they have the impudence even to think? Peter concludes with a deprecation of those who assail the state and the court—a means of mockery since it pretends to condone vice among the nobility.

"A Second Epistle to Mrs. Clarke" begins with the news that
the duke has quit his post and has retired to the country. Peter
then says that few deserve the favor of fortune and adds that some
people would claim they were poor though they possessed the wealth
of Mexico—an implication that the duke has received and retained
bribes. With awkward transitions, Peter next damns Mrs. Clarke,
praises the Prince of Wales, and speaks against reformers who destroy the good, Mrs. Clarke's beauty, while destroying the bad:

> What madness centres in that word "reform!"
> Who would destroy a *garden* for a *worm*?
> Who, but a Bedlamite, would fire his house,
> To wreck his vengeance on a pilfering mouse?   (ll. 97–100)

Mockingly, the satirist asks why reformers should want to banish
Bribery which circulates gold and buys votes:

> What beauteous Insects from *corruption* spring;
> Leave humble dirt, and sport the gilded wing!
> What Flowers of vivid hue, and rich perfume,
> To *stable-litter* owe their balm and bloom!   (ll . 113–16)

Censure should then be silent even though there might soon be babes
on the army list, perhaps even children yet unborn. These reformers
are tyrants who achieved power through spurious fanaticism. The
imps are saints on Sundays and devils the rest of the week; with one
eye, they look to God; with the other, wink at the Devil. They teach
charity to the poor, but they kick the beggar from their door. Such
actions by reformers should warn the fair lady that these hypocrites
might "thy paths pursue;/ And hunt thee to the bed of lawless
blisses" (ll. 170–71). If she were caught, she should not plead for
mercy, since mercy does not know where reformers dwell. Thus
Peter ends the satire; and he hopes that, if the sovereign likes it,
George will offer him a place or a pension.

The *Epistles to Mrs. Clarke* are Peter Pindar's worst satires;
they lack the wit, the sparkle, the jollity which characterizes most
of his work; they are poorly conceived and poorly constructed; for
Peter lashes but doesn't seem to know where or at whom to strike.
Declining popularity and falling sales may have had a bearing in
reducing his effectiveness, or his sympathy may have been with the
lady and not her accusers. One salient point is evident: Peter Pindar
felt that corrupt individuals should not establish themselves as

judges. Only a general house cleaning could accomplish the purification ceremony necessary for good government, and the process should be a gradual and a sane one.

V *George IV*

The Prince of Wales became regent in February, 1811, when it became obvious that George III would not recover from his insanity attack of 1810.   After a year as regent, he assumed full control of affairs and was nominally king until his father's death, at which time he bacame George IV. The prince gave a sumptuous party at Carlton House when he became regent; and John Wolcot appears to have thought he might receive a pension or some other sinecure because he had often complimented the free-spending prince in his satires. Wolcot was disappointed in this hope and was not even invited to the prince's festivities. The poet's chagrin is presented in *Carlton-House Fête; or the Disappointed Bard; in a Series of Elegies; to which is added, Curiosity in Rags; an Elegy* (1811). Age may have made Peter Pindar realize that such lack of gratitude is the way of the world, for these six elegies in four-line stanzas of varying length feature no bitterness, or his presentation of mock sorrow may have meant he still hoped through these poems to obtain a monetary reward. The hope was vain, and the matter was dropped.

In "Elegy I," which contains eighteen four-line stanzas, the unnoticed, unrewarded, and therefore grief-stricken poet sits on the bank of the Thames. Only one ray has pierced his gloom: the great display "Of Eastern Grandeur at the Prince's Fête" (1. 8), for at the fête he wouldn't be forgotten, and he eagerly awaits a letter of invitation. The ten stanzas which follow, each beginning with "Sharp as . . . ," record his anxiety; he awaited word "sharp as" a maid expecting a poet's letters of lovesick sighs, or as a kite hoping to feed on barnyard fowls, or,

> Sharp as a Bailiff for a hiding debtor;
>   Or as the hard Churchwarden on the poor;
> Or bilious Critic on a word, or letter,
>   To scalp his victim author o'er and o'er.   (ll. 21–24)

Thus, exalting in hope, he said, if he were made the master of the horse, he wouldn't care. To every imagined knock on the door,

Fancy made him think a royal compliment would appear addressed to him. He just knew he would soon be dining at Carlton House.

"Elegy II", of twenty four-line stanzas, opens with the poet's asking if he must weep. There may be goldfish at Carlton House, but he has no gold, nor a grain of favor; and he is the example of rewarded loyalty. What is even more mortifying about his not being invited is that those in charge of issuing invitations had invited twenty dead people. Peter had often dined with Weltjie, the prince's cook; and the prince should blush because he hasn't followed the cook's example. If Peter can, he will honor the cook by giving to the gossip-loving public Weltjie's memoirs. "Elegy III," fifteen stanzas, proclaims that, before Peter's poems were sold, copies were sent to the prince; and the satirist finds it strange that he should now be forgotten. If he had been invited, he would have immortalized through verse each guest and shown posterity the treat. His account would have been far better than the languid prose of the newspapers. He concludes that Oblivion is ever ready "To sink a name or a virtue in a pool" (1.60).

The seven stanzas of "Elegy IV" suggest table decorations which should have been a part of the prince's entertainment. There should have been a washtub with paper ships representing the Trafalgar and Nile battles and a baker's tray of gingerbread soldiers cutting the French in two. These suggestions subtly indicate that frivolity has made the prince forget to whom he owes his position and that England may have forgotten that a war is still being fought. In the seven stanzas of "Elegy V," the most pointed and the best of *Carlton-House Fete,* Pindar asks his Muse why he was omitted from the festivities and wonders if Dame Fitzherbert, the discarded wife and mistress of the prince, illustrates what one could expect from the man. In favor once, she indulged in a dream; and the poet is in disfavor because he wished her happier days. There was a time when a nod or a smile blessed the poet, when he felt that his room would float with wine and oil from a patron. Too soon his hopes lost their bloom, and he discovered that no meaning can be attached to the nod or the smile. Well, he must simply wait longer for Fortune. If he hanged himself, no tear would be forced from Carlton-House.

The fourteen stanzas of "Curiosity in Rags" which conclude these lamentations describe the melee which ensued when the general public was admitted to Carlton House after the festivities were over. The push, crush, and shove of the curious produced many evils;

petticoats were torn, bonnets and shoes were lost, as well as necklaces and bracelets. Women displayed much of themselves freely, and the crowd was so great that many a fainting girl had to be helped from the rooms. Soon girls lost all of their clothing and went home covered with aprons, sheets, or tablecloths. Slyly Peter concludes with a mock compliment to the prince's morals. After describing the dishabille of the women, he exclaims, "Pray God, the *modest* Regent did not view it!" (1. 56).

Only praise can be accorded *Carlton-House Fete*. Peter Pindar rises above his feelings of neglect and self-pity and does not vociferously denounce the regent. Briefly, clearly, and simply, he states his case: he has been unrewarded for past compliments; he had expected much and was disappointed. Resigned to his lot, he has shown that one should not expect much from the Prince of Wales, that a nod or a smile may mean nothing. A few subtle thrusts at the prince's morality are given, but good-humored wit prevails. Viewed in its entirety, *Carlton-House Fete* is a refreshing piece after Peter's poorly conceived and structured previous publication, the *Epistles to Mrs. Clarke*.

VI *Chinese Travelers*

Wolcot's last published satire, one not included in his collected works, is *A Most Solemn and Important Epistle to the Emperor of China: On His Uncourtly and Impolitic Behavior to the Sublime Ambassadors of Great Britain* (1817). The thirty-two, six-line stanzas of this satire are the only ones with John Wolcot's real name attached to them as the author. A period of six years had passed since his last satire; and his imitators, particularly C.F. Lowlar, were now using the name Peter Pindar. A clear identification of the author of the piece had now to be made, but it was known that John Wolcot was the creator of Peter Pindar. In this, his last known satire, John Wolcot in his late seventies shows no signs of senility as he once again writes a topical satire.

After the peace of 1815, the British government could deal with the complaints of English merchants at Canton over the exactions made upon them by Chinese mandarins. William Pitt Amherst (1737-1857) was appointed envoy to the Chinese Emperor Kea K'ing; and, in February, 1816, he set sail for China, arriving in Canton in July.[11] Amherst journeyed to the city of Tientsin, then to T'ung-chow, and arrived on August 29, 1816, at the palace of Yuen-ming-yuen where he was immediately called to attend the emperor; but, due to fatigue from his journey, Amherst declined. He was ordered to leave immediately, and he returned back to Canton on January 20, 1817, from where he set sail for England.[12] Sir George Thomas Staunton (1781–1859), who had accompanied his father on the first visit of 1792, was also a member of the commission to Peking and was probably one of the few individuals in the party who could speak Chinese.[13]

The earliest account of the embassy, besides that of George Ellis's *Journal of the Late Embassy to China,* which appeared near the end of 1817, is that given by a correspondent signing himself "D. T." in the *Gentleman's Magazine* for September, 1817 (231–32). "D. T.'s" account contains the information given in the preceding paragraph but offers one additional fact: the viceroy of Canton threatened to fire on the *Alceste* and *Lyra* if the ships entered the Tigris River. The ships went ahead, were fired upon, and the *Alceste* fired back, driving the Chinese out of their battery, which ensured a safe voyage (232). Wolcot's *Epistle to the Emperor of China* finds the satirist unable to fathom the rash Chinese actions since England, reflecting the regent's tastes, was engaging in a mania for Chinese decor. Mister Nash, the prince's decorator, has even transformed Carlton House into a Mandarin's home:

> Know, we were growing all *Chinese*—
> Nought but the Eastern style could please,—
> Witness the glittering gold Pavilion rooms;
>   Where (for the noses of the Great,
>   His HIGHNESS may vouchsafe to treat)
> Snakes of a size enormous puff perfumes.   (ll. 19–24)

The desire for Chinese decor has even changed the standards of beauty, for brilliant blue or sparkling coal-black eyes are not the fashion "But eyes that seem the light to shun,/ Just like a cat's before the Sun" (ll. 46–47). Furthermore,

> The *Roman* nose, a comely feature,
> And celebrated work of Nature,
> Had by a *snub* been robb'd of just renown;
>   The cheek with ruddy health that glows,
>   Whose blushes emulate the rose,
> Had mourn'd the triumph of *dirty brown*.   (ll. 49–54)

The ample white bosom of the maid is no longer displayed, the large foot has given way to the petite, and the beaux at court have pulled their beards out by the roots. Music has given way to "Tremendous solos from the mighty *Gong*!" (1.84). The recent Chinese actions will now cause another change in taste and the pagoda at Kew no longer please the eye.

Imagining the ship's blushing at her treatment as she journeys from Peking, he warns the emperor of Britain's power, a reference to the *Alceste*, for "Thou knowest what One ship could do" (l. 152). Moreover, the Chinese ruler should remember what England did to France and Napoleon. If Chinese ambassadors had come to England, they would have received fair treatment. Wolcot closes with some mockery about the value of his verse: "Kings are ambitious of my song;/ But mark, Successor of Kien Long,/ First mend *thy* manners, ere thou gain'st *my* praise" (ll. 190–92).

Wolcot appends a "Moral Reflection on the Foregoing Epistle," and the four lines have a bite only if applied to the prince regent also:

> It is a very easy thing
> Inded, to make a man a *King*;
> But, since the reign of Kings began,
> How hard to make a *King a Man*!

This last satire by Wolcot offers his usual methods and attitudes: the attention to detail, the creeping-in of British nationalism, the jibes at folly associated with the taste for Chinese decor, and the hint of the defender of British liberty. The humor and the wit are still fresh, though some doggerel occasionally creeps in. But Wolcot closed his career with a poem which accounts for his decline into obscurity—he has written another topical satire.

CHAPTER 11

Literary Techniques and Evaluation

I Literary Techniques

JOHN Wolcot's primary satirical method is, as has been stated, that of reportage: he is the chatty columnist printing gossip and offering either advice or warnings. He selected his materials from incidents in his personal experience or from contemporary events. Social events were only obliquely dealt with, for, more than anything else, John Wolcot was a dealer in personalities. Anyone publicly prominent was fair game for him, but he chose the most prominent for his major satires and mentioned others only briefly. He aimed and shot at the big game, but he wounded the smaller with brief references within a satire. The majority of Wolcot's selections betray him as climbing on a bandwagon or as following traditional materials as in his caricatures of the king and of other political figures; George III, however, became Peter Pindar's special province.

Wolcot examines and belittles his victim because the latter cannot see how foolish or how far lost in folly he is. He asks him to use reason and clear eyesight; to be realistic and to follow nature. He appeals always to reason, common sense, decorum, and even moderation. Egotism must be banished from the victim who might be brought to his senses by a wry suggestion that he continue in his foolish endeavors. A funhouse mirror is placed before the victim; the mirror distorts the figure but might make him go on a diet and sup at the frugal table of reason and common sense. General good, not private good, is advocated, especially in connection with the satires on politicians; for a politician should represent and work for the people. George III, however, represents the nation and should act like a proper king. The satirist is critical, but he is fair.

As for the techniques Peter Pindar employed, he presents himself as an honest person with no ulterior motives except the public good and improvement. He points out that he is no coarse, brutal Churchill, Pope, or Swift; he is mild and good humored. He masquerades as the urbane gentleman who corrects but who knows the way of the world. If his lash bites, it may do some good; for doing good also means that one learns to praise or to flatter only those who are actually worthy of esteem. As the disinterested protector of reason's reign and as the castigator of folly, Peter Pindar claims his satire will cease once the person in error comes to his senses.

To achieve his intent, Wolcot uses many devices, and the most prominent is mock praise conveyed through mock panegyric or mock epithet, followed frequently by an anticlimactic thrust, as in his statement that the world reads Bruce's *Travels* with feelings of astonishment—and wonders if any of it is true. The term "gentleman" may be italicized, and the context reveals the phrase to be an empty title since Wolcot means quite the opposite. He compares his subject with a lofty or a low figure to bring his victim into closer perspective and to undercut his pride: George III's anger is as threatening as Jove's, but the object of such wrath is not worth all the uproar; Thomas Paine is a raven, a bird of ill omen. This method seeks to establish value frames for the reader and to cause the victim to blush.

One of the most frequent comparisons made by the satirist is, as has been noted, that of persons to animals: Pitt may drink as much as Dundas, but Dundas gets as drunk as a pig. Antiquarians and archeologists labor and dig like moles without the aid of light (the light of reason and common sense). The "bluestockings" are tigers as critics—tigers with sharp claws ready to pounce. England is a cow almost milked dry by milkman Pitt. Pindar often uses the metaphor of the pig-like snout of the victim to reveal folly.

Another comparative device is the use of the fable or tale to illustrate a truth or to make a point. Wolcot takes some of Aesop's fables—such as the frogs who desire a king, the marriage between diverse animals, the peacock's vanity, the vain stag, and Hercules and the carter—to reveal lack of sense; people do not know what they want, nor do they know when they are fortunate. Jean de la Fontaine's pieces—the cat turned into a lady, the young widow who forgets her vow of perpetual mourning, and the monkey who talks a cat into pulling chestnuts from a fire—are used to reveal that a person's nature is difficult to change, that vows are fragile things, and that the public should beware of sweet-talking politicians. And far better are Peter Pindar's own tales and fables such as "The Apple Dumplings and the King" that reveals George III's foolishness, or "The Magpie and the Robin" that discloses the horror of Paine's message to the world.

Wolcot's metaphors are sometimes faulty; if writers are unjustly attacked by critics, he says writer's minds should sit calmly on their thrones; if people want him to change his style, he calls it misplaced labor to attempt to wash an ass's face. The awkward images in these examples might indicate haste in composition and no revision.

He used quotations and italics constantly. The quotations have already been discussed as a reporter's technique, but the italics serve to underline a point, to highlight it. But he overuses italics; the effect of wit is lessened when the reader is plainly directed to, forced to, see a jest. Instead of discovering and marveling at the author's cleverness, the reader accepts it and passes on.

Parody, pun, burlesque, and lampoon all play their part in Peter Pindar's satires. Suspense is created by withholding the punch line until the end of a verse sentence and suspicion is aroused by doubting the satiric victim's veracity. At his best, Wolcot used many details for pictorial effects as in *The Royal Tour* with its marvelously crowded and animated presentation of animal onlookers who watch, not without danger, George III begin his journey to Weymouth. Details are also used to accumulate evidence against a subject as seen by the anecdotes uttered by Johnson's biographers in *Bozzy and Piozzi*. The numerous details give Wolcot's verse vitality and interest; the lack of them, especially in the political satires, makes the verse lifeless.

As a versifier, John Wolcot understood metrics. His heroic couplets are well executed despite a tendency to use a dactyl instead of an iamb at the beginning of a line. His odes are usually composed of six-line stanzas, four lines in iambic tetrameter, and two in iambic pentameter; and variety is achieved with some anapests. What is faulty in his lines results from adhering too closely to a stress pattern at times and utilizing any word or words to fit the pattern; too much use of "Oh," "And lo," "But oh," and "Alas" appears; and these become dull and deadening to anyone who would critically read all of his verse. Also doggerel creeps into his lines, and it is not used for parody but for the sake of rhyme or for a quick way to state something. A lack of imagination or perhaps a lack of creative ability accounts for this doggerel verse; a more creative poet would have been able to express the ideas in a manner which would earn a discriminating reader's praise and not his censure.

Yet Peter Pindar's style is always clear, always concise, and mostly good humored. The reader is not presented with circumlocutions, inverted sentences, or witticisms that seem strained and artificial. His clarity of expression and his colloquial manner are important factors in success, but these alone do not make a successful writer. The basic reason he was widely read seems to be that Peter Pindar was amusing; he could tell a good joke, such as the one about the lost jackass and the laxative pill or about Sir Joseph Banks and the boiled fleas. He vividly presents amusing anecdotes about the famous, such as George III's visits to brewery and hovel. He could humorously reveal royal parsimony in readily discerned, descriptive images: the hearth crickets in the royal household have colds and rheumatisms. In part, therefore, Pindar was successful because he amused and very rarely disappointed his audience.

Wolcot's appeal lay also in his attacks on the famous and in his questioning the meaning of success in a particular profession. He humanized the famous by making them foolish through caricature, and his public could read and feel that they were superior in some respects to these figures. Moreover, people can more readily and wholeheartedly laugh at a joke that is not at their expense. If Peter Pindar occasionally used a slightly vulgar word or expression, this made him more human, more common. There is a shock value to such words; they can create a desired effect similar to a political cartoonist's exaggeration of a candidate's nose; and the prints of Wolcot's times, the Rowlandson and the Gilray caricatures, startled viewers in a like manner. Wolcot's exaggerated examples of one specific man's foolishness would be apparent to the least knowledgeable reader; his irony would appeal to the more discerning members in his audience. He followed no particular party, and each reader could view him as a co-partisan. He also won his audience by presenting himself as a tickler with a feather, not as one who prods with a razor or a knife. Wolcot was like the genial guest whom one invites to dinner because one knows his pleasantries about current events will produce a lively evening.

Certain motifs appear constantly. His attitude toward fallen women and prostitutes is that of the sentimental humanitarian; woman's fall is a result of her beauty, and the seducer—not the seduced—should receive all the blame and shame. Time is viewed as the destroyer of beauty and of reputations; it is useless to fight time, but all men wish to arrest its movement. In respect to religion, Wolcot felt that hypocrisy on the public's part motivated piety. People pray for one hour on Sunday and pretend they are Christians;

the rest of the time they follow their inclinations and emotions. Hypocrisy for Wolcot was a capital sin practiced most frequently by churchgoers and churchmen. As for liberty and freedom, he favored the common man *and* the monarchy. Though he stated that the king and the commoner were equal, he also said that kings have a purpose but should not be dictators. As for marriage, he saw that in many cases it was a farce when two people lived together in incompatibility and when one party wanted the other dead; the honeymoon and love were soon over.

What must be considered Wolcot's major motif, whether stated directly or indirectly, is his attitude toward mankind. Man is very stupid, full of pride, lacking in sense, stubborn in his refusal to follow reason and common sense, and fond of variety. Passion, a title, or the relegation of the intellect to only a small aspect of life which does not deal with individuals in society causes man to forget Christian teachings and the actual conditions of the world. The world of man does not want to think; it wants the variety which does not give people time to examine or to meditate on life. The populace, in Peter Pindar's view, is like a group of starlings who alight on cow droppings and then rush off to banquet on horse droppings; the problem is that the world does not realize that the diet is still the same and is certainly not wholesome or the best of fare.

II   *Summation*

In John Wolcot and his works, we find a man of some talent, talent in a satirical vein, who does not heighten his poetry through careful composition. Perhaps he was lazy and was satisfied with the first word instead of a better one. A versifier with some talent and potential, he relegated his abilities to the area of topical satire. His desire to accumulate money led him to repeat a financially successful attack on an individual, and therefore his sincerity can be questioned. When a subject began to pall, such as the satires on the royal academicians, he changed his topic. But his better qualities, his clarity, his good-natured humor, and his pictorial ability should be applauded despite the fact that, in the last analysis, he emerged as a satirical writer of ability who, basing his work on the contemporary scene, soon lapsed from public favor and was read only by a select group of students of eighteenth-century English literature.

Humorous, witty, urbane, John Wolcot lost his vogue by concentrating on a specific individual's folly instead of on universal elements in man. If types rather than specific individuals had been presented, the satires might have achieved more respect and more fame—but fewer sales. But Wolcot's choice and his method were to so gear his satires to an individual's personality and to his times that only with effort and by disregarding major aspects of the work could they be considered to have universality. They are, as he presents them, historical eccentrics who cannot stand for all men. They remain of the earth and of the past; one can never forget that they are figures in history. Wolcot's satires must, therefore, be praised for what they are and for what they illustrate: public figures and history of the last two decades of eighteenth-century and the first decade of nineteenth-century England.

Despite this muted praise of Wolcot and his works, a study of the man and his satires is still worthwhile, as a brief examination of Wolcot's position in English literary history reveals. W. J. Courthorpe uses Peter Pindar as the prime illustration for "the decline of Satire in ethical quality, with its increasing tendency to become unreservedly personal and scandalous."[1] C. W. Previte-Orton says, "He was a born humorist and the very best of English caricaturists in verse."[2] Although W. L. Renwick calls him "the grand mouthpiece of English vulgarity," he adds that "Peter Pindar was indeed something of an institution, the English Philistine, too much determined to be nobody's fool, but, if sometimes annoying, sometimes tiresome, no great menace to anybody. Peter Pindars have their uses; they help to keep us from getting too solemn, and a little of their cheerful blackguardism is a corrective of oppressive dignity."[3] Kenneth Hopkins considers Pindar "the greatest master of verse caricature in English, perhaps the only one of consequence."[4] Grzegorz Sinko regards him as even more important: "The point, however, seems to be, that if we want to consider the development of English satire as a more or less continuous process, Wolcot's name emerges as the most significant one in the decades between Churchill and Byron, not merely (as is the case with the *Rolliad* or the 'Anti-Jacobin') as an isolated literary fact, but as a link between two generations and, at the same time, as a representative spokesman of his period, which was neither short nor unimportant."[5]

So Peter Pindar can be viewed as a reflection of his age, a man who footnotes history. His view of his contemporaries stands as a general view of the period by the man in the street. His views of literary figures, especially the more famous, aid one to understand the literature written during the period. Though these views concerning historical significance will ensure that Wolcot has a place, a role, or a function in literary history, he is still worthwhile to study for another reason. Wolcot's works can be read because he is effective, because he is amusing, and because he is clever and witty. He approachs universality but does not reach it; but does this lack matter? One can mine him for what is valuable, and the excavations will not be for naught. As one works, his humor, his cleverness, and his wit lighten the tunnel's path. Though others promise amusement and don't redeem the promise, Wolcot offers it and delivers it in abundance.

Wolcot established no school, he probably influenced no writers, but he did have imitators. He was not unique; other satirists such as existed during his period wrote about the same subjects he did. So he could be labeled as a minor satirist of the eighteenth century who had a brief vogue and was forgotten; but to so label him would mean a loss of Wolcot's cleverness and wit—for few want to read anyone labeled "minor writer." Evaluation and comparison with other writers may place Wolcot's work low on a scale of values; but he, on the same scale, is above others and has more value than others. He is not so great as Juvenal and Pope, but he is greater than such of his contemporaries as Thomas Mathias and William Gifford; he has value and is gifted. To read Peter Pindar's works is to discover his times, the last two decades of the eighteenth century, a period lacking in greatness; and John Wolcot's works and the man are apt representatives of the period. Reading Peter Pindar's satires will not be toil, for a reader, like General Kosciusko, will find in Pindar something to sustain him.

Notes and References

Chapter One

1. John Taylor, *Records of My Life* (London, 1932), I, 239n.
2. Edward Collins Giddy, "A Biographical Sketch of the late Doctor John Wolcot (Peter Pindar) Interspersed with Extracts from some of his Letters." MS in Falmouth Public Library, Cornwall, England.
3. Giddy MS.
4. Taylor, II, 240.
5. Richard Polwhele, *Traditions and Recollections* (London, 1826), p. 37.
6. Giddy MS.
7. Ada Earland, *John Opie and His Circle* (London, 1911), p. 14.
8. *Ibid.*, p. 29.
9. Leslie Stephen in *DNB*, s.v. "William Mason."
10. A. S. Collins, *The Profession of Letters* (New York, 1929), p. 92.
11. Giddy MS.
12. William Carr in *DNB*, s.v. "John Wolcot."
13. *Annual Biography and Obituary for the Year 1820*, IV, 320.
14. Mary Shelley, *Journal*, ed. Frederick L. Jones (Norman, Oklahoma, 1948), p. 65.
15. *Ibid.*, p. 80.
16. Taylor, II, 237.

Chapter Two

1. William Sandby, *The History of the Royal Academy of Arts* (London, 1862), I, 49.
2. Miles F. DeMontmorency, *A Short History of Painting in England* (London, 1933), p. 111; John Rothenstein, *An Introduction to English Painting* (London, 1933), p. 82.
3. DeMontmorency, p. 121.
4. Rothenstein, p. 107.
5. DeMontmorency, p. 112.
6. Sandby, I, 253–64.
7. *Works of Peter Pindar* (London, 1812), Vol. II, p. 381.

Chapter Three

1. Horace Walpole, *Letters,* edited by Mrs. Paget Toynbee (Oxford, 1905), XIII, 372.

2. *Ibid.,* p. 375.

3. P. M. Zall, "Peter Pindar, 'Redividus,'" *Notes and Queries* (July 19, 1952), p. 320.

4. George Saintsbury, *Essays in English Literature: 1780–1860* (New York, 1895), p. 254.

5. Edmund Kemper Broadus, *The Laureatship* (Oxford, 1921), p. 150.

6. Kenneth Hopkins, *The Poets Laureate* (New York, 1955), pp. 92–96.

7. *Ibid.,* p. 105.

8. *Ibid.,* p. 109.

9. *Ibid.,* p. 115.

10. W. Forbes Gray, *The Poets Laureate of England* (New York, 1915), p. 205.

11. Broadus, p. 154.

12. *Works of Peter Pindar* (London, 1812), V, 309.

13. Horace Walpole, *Correspondence,* edited by W. S. Lewis (New Haven and London, 1961), XXXI, 255; a similar view is presented in *The Georgian Era* (London, 1834), III, 39.

14. Richard Garnett in *DNB,* s.v. "James Bruce."

15. M. G. Jones, *Hannah More* (Cambridge, England, 1952), p. 15.

16. *Ibid.,* p. 120.

Chapter Four

1. Dorothy Stinson, *Scientists and Amateurs* (New York, 1948), p. 27.

2. Norman Pearson, "The Virtuosi," *The Nineteenth Century* (November, 1908), LXVI, 859.

3. Stinson, pp. 70–92.

4. *Ibid.,* p. 148.

5. Hector Charles Cameron, *Sir Joseph Banks* (London, 1952), pp. 1–64; Benjamin Daydon Jackson in *DNB,* s.v. "Sir Joseph Banks."

6. Stinson, p. 172.

7. Cameron, p. 113.

8. Sir Henry Lyons, *The Royal Society: 1660–1940* (Cambridge, England, 1944), pp. 198–211.

9. Edward Smith, *The Life of Sir Joseph Banks* (London and New York, 1911), pp. 94–96.

10. Jackson in *DNB.*

11. Cameron, p. 271.

12. Warwick William Worth in *DNB* s.v. "Sir William Hamilton."

13. George Paul Macdonnell in *DNB* s.v. "Daines Barrington."

14. Robert Harrison in *DNB* s.v. "Sir Charles Blagden."

15. James Alden Thompson, *Count Rumford of Massachusetts* (New York, 1935); W.J. Sparrow, *Count Rumford of Woburn, Mass.* (New York, 1965); William Fraser Rae in *DNB* s.v. "Sir Benjamin Thompson."

16. Rae in *DNB;* "Historical Chronicle" of the *Annual Register* for 1800, p. 6.

17. Rae in *DNB.*

18. Thompson, p. 96.

19. *Ibid.,* p. 110.

20. *Ibid.,* p. xvi.

21. Sparrow, p. 259.

22. George Thomas Bettany in *DNB* s.v. "James Graham."

Chapter Five

1. *Works of Peter Pindar* (London, 1812), V, 269.

2. Austin Dobson, "A Literary Printer," *Robala's Journal and Other Papers* (London, 1915), p. 198.

3. George Atherton Aitkin in *DNB,* s.v. "John Nichols." See also "Memoirs of John Nichols, Esq., F.S.A." in *Gentleman's Magazine,* December, 1826, pp. 489–504.

4. Dobson, p. 225.

5. *Works of Peter Pindar* (London, 1794), II, 242n.

6. *Works of Peter Pindar* (London, 1812), V, 229–230.

7. *Works* (1812), V, 229n.

8. *Ibid.,* IV, 135.

Chapter Six

1. Tom Girtin, *Doctor with Two Aunts* (London, 1959), p. 25.

2. W.E. Woodward, *Tom Paine: America's Godfather* (New York, 1945), p. 188; see also, Ramsay Muir, *A Short History of the British Commonwealth* (London, 1949), II, 164–66; G. M. Trevelyan, *English Social History* (London, 1942), pp. 468 and 482.

3. Woodward, p. 211.

4. Woodward, p. 222; see also R. R. Fennessy, *Burke, Paine, and the Rights of Man: A Difference of Political Opinion* (The Hague, 1963), pp. 241–43.

5. J. Steven Watson, *The Reign of George III: 1760–1815* (Oxford, England, 1960), p. 324.

6. Woodward, p. 218.

7. *Ibid.,* p. 218.

8. *Ibid.,* p. 233; Fennessy, p. 244.

9. Woodward, pp. 199 and 205.

10. *Works of Peter Pindar* (London, 1812), II, 479.

11. *Ibid.,* III, 261.

12. Watson, p. 360.

13. *Works* (1816), IV, 421–29.

Chapter Seven

1. John W. Derry, *William Pitt* (London, 1962), pp. 9–13; William Hunt in *DNB,* s.v. "William Pitt."

2. Derry, p. 72.

3. *Ibid.,* pp. 19 and 136.

4. *Ibid.,* p. 73; Hunt in *DNB.*

5. Donald Grove Barnes, *George III and William Pitt, 1783–1806* (Stanford and London, 1939), pp. 182–89; Derry, pp. 63–69.

6. Philip Ziegler, *Addington* (New York, 1965), p. 39.

7. Barnes, p. 182; Derry, pp. 68–69.

8. Derry, p. 47.

9. Thomas Wright, *Caricature History of the Georges* (London, 1867), pp. 494–95.

10. Barnes, p. 309.

11. Barnes, p. 309; for a similar account of the bill's contents see J. Steven Watson, *The Reign of George III: 1760–1815* (Oxford, England, 1960), p. 360.

12. Derry, pp. 22, 27, and 48; Barnes, p. 306.

13. Derry, p. 103.

14. *Works of Peter Pindar* (London, 1812), III, 403.

15. Derry, p. 110.

16. Robert Huish, *Memoirs of George the Third* (London, 1821), p. 602.

17. *Works* (1812), III, 460.

18. Derry, p. 136; Barnes, pp. 343–46 and 381.

19. Watson, pp. 402 and 417; Ziegler, *Addington.*

20. *The Times* (London), November 23, 1802, p. 3; November 30, 1802, p. 3.

21. *Works* (1812), V, 226.

22. *Ibid.,* V, 228.

23. *Ibid.,* IV, 527–28.

24. Barnes, pp. 443 and 467; Hunt in *DNB.*

25. *Works* (1812), V, 276.

26. *Ibid.,* V, 226.

Chapter Eight

1. Robert Huish, *Memoirs of George the Third* (London, 1821); Manfred S. Guttmacher, *America's Last King* (New York, 1941); William Hunt in *DNB* s.v. "George III."

2. Huish, pp. 99–107.

3. *Ibid.,* pp. 673–85; Guttmacher, pp. 365–77.

4. Guttmacher, p. 176.

5. Huish, p. 333.

6. Guttmacher, p. 242.

7. *Ibid.,* p. 173.

8. Huish, p. 343.

9. Thomas Wright, *Caricature History of the Georges* (London, England; 1867), p. 414.

10. Guttmacher, p. 176.

11. Huish, p. 380.

12. Guttmacher, p. 175.

13. Huish, p. 460.

14. *Ibid.,* p. 265.

15. *Ibid.,* p. 265.

16. *Ibid.,* p. 483.

17. *Ibid.,* p. 483.

18. *Ibid.,* p. 483.

19. Guttmacher, p. 177.

20. *Gentleman's Magazine* (May, 1786), p. 442.

21. *Ibid.,* May, 1786, pp. 437–38.

22. Huish, p. 554.

23. *Ibid.,* p. 541. Guttmacher, p. 255, says the date was June 24, 1789.

24. Huish, p. 589.

Chapter Nine

1. Robert Huish, *Memoirs of George the Third* (London, 1821), pp. 461–63.

2. *Ibid.,* pp. 461–62.

3. *Ibid.,* p. 465.

4. *Works of Peter Pindar* (London, 1812), I, 171.

5. *Ibid.,* I, 202.

6. Agnes Mary Clerke in *DNB* s.v. "Sir William Herschel."

Chapter Ten

1. George Fisher Russell Baker in *DNB,* s.v. "James Lowther"; *Gentleman's Magazine* (June, 1802), pp. 568–88, s.v. "James Lowther."

2. Baker in *DNB.*

3. *Gentleman's Magazine* (June, 1802), p. 587.

4. Tom Girtin, *Doctor with Two Aunts* (London, 1959), p. 147.

5. Henry Manners Chichester in *DNB,* s.v. "George Macartney"; see also Chapter 9 of William W. Appleton's *A Cycle of Cathay: The Chinese*

Vogue in England during the Seventeenth and Eighteenth Centuries (New York, 1951).

6. Chichester in *DNB*.

7. Henry Morse Stephens in *DNB*, s.v. "Mary Anne Clarke"; *Gentleman's Magazine* (August, 1802), pp. 208–9.

8. Stephens in *DNB*.

9. *Ibid.*

10. Roger Fulford, *George the Fourth* (London, 1929), p. 78.

11. Robert Kennaway Douglas in *DNB*, s.v. "William Pitt Amherst."

12. *Ibid.*

13. George Clement Boase in *DNB*, s.v. "Sir George Thomas Staunton."

Chapter Eleven

1. W. J. Courthorpe, *A History of English Poetry* (London, 1905) V, 244.

2. C. W. Previte Orton, *Political Satire in English Poetry* (Cambridge, England; 1910), pp. 147–48.

3. W. L. Renwick, *English Literature: 1789–1815* (Oxford, England; 1963), pp. 47 and 113–14.

4. Kenneth Hopkins, *Portraits in Satire* (London, 1958), p. 217.

5. Grzegorz Sinko, *John Wolcot and His School, A Chapter from the History of English Satire* (Wroclaw, 1962), p. 105.

Selected Bibliography

PRIMARY SOURCES

I. Works by Peter Pindar

(ed.) *The Beauties of English Poetry*. London: C. Spelsbury and J. Walker, 1804.

The Fall of Portugal; or, the Royal Exiles. London: Longman, Hurst, Rees, Orme and Walker, 1808.

A Most Solemn and Important Epistle to the Emperor of China. London: Walker and Edwards, 1817.

Persian Love Elegies. Kingston, Jamaica: Joseph Thompson, 1773.

Peter Pindar's Poems, selected by P. M. Zall with a Foreword by A. L. Rowse (University of South Carolina Press, 1972). Very brief introduction to author. Contains twenty-four poems, including *Epistle to James Boswell* and Part I of *Bozzy and Piozzi*.

Poems Selected from the Works of Peter Pindar, Esquire. New York: T. B. Jensen, 1804.

The Poetical Works of Peter Pindar, Esquire. Philadelphia: W. Spotswood and Rice and Co., 1789.

The Works of Peter Pindar. 3 vols. London: John Walker, 1794.

The Works of Peter Pindar. 4 vols. Boston: Charles Williams, 1811.

The Works of Peter Pindar. 5 vols. London: J. Walker, 1812.

————. 1816 edition.

The Works of Peter Pindar, Esq. with a Copious Index. London: Jones and Company, 1824.

II. Works Attributed to John Wolcot

The Cambridge Bibliography of English Literature lists three works by John Wolcot which, I believe, are either not his or else were partially written by him: *Tales and Fables, A Letter to the Most Insolent Man Alive,* and *The Cap*. The reasons for this opinion are given below where each work is examined separately, but of major importance is that none of them was included in any collected edition of Peter Pindar's works although all three were published before Robinson, Goulding, and Walker brought out the editions.

Tales and Fables (London: T. Hookham, 1788) does not bear any author's name and was not published by Kearsly, Wolcot's first publisher. In this sixty-three-page quarto pamphlet are two tales and twenty fables whose moral is either implicit or, most frequently, given to the reader. These stories deal with sentimental generalities on life, man, and fame. One example of the style and commonplaces will suffice. In Fable II, "Marian and the Garland," the girl weaves a garland of flowers in the morning and by evening the leaves have faded. The garland speaks, saying that its fading warns Marian of her own future:

> And since the doom awaits thee too
>   To flourish but an hour,
> By modest worth, and feeling true,
>   Be plac'd beyond its power.   (ll. 21–24)

The lack of wit, compression, originality of sentiments, and ironic twists and turns makes it doubtful as to its being written by Wolcot.

A Letter to the Most Insolent Man Alive (London: G. Kearsley, 1789) has no author's name after its title. This prose letter in thirty-one quarto pages is signed "An Englishman" and deals with the regency question of the period. When Wolcot attacked a person, he named the person. In this prose piece, William Pitt is not referred to by name; furthermore, it lacks the humor and wit which Wolcot lavished on his subject when he abandoned verse for prose. Another indication that Wolcot was not the writer lies in the sincere compliments to the king and queen. Allowances are made for the queen because she labors under "sorrow for the calamity of the best of husbands" (10). Wolcot would have praised the royal family only to state or to imply the opposite; in short, his compliments would not be compliments at all.

The Cap "by Peter Pindar" (London: printed for the Author, 1795) is a forty-one-page satire in heroic couplets on dramatic writers of the day. In this work, Folly appears with a cap and bells (fool's cap) to bestow on the dullest dramatic writer of the period. Thirty-four dramatists are mentioned with such a lack of concise, biting metaphors or epithets to describe them that it is doubtful that Wolcot could have written this satire of little wit, less humor, and much that is predictable. Furthermore, Richard Cumberland is praised, the dramatist whom Wolcot damned in Canto III of *The Lousiad* (1791).

I believe that these three pieces were not written by John Wolcot since they lack those humorous and ironic elements and metaphors taken from everyday life that are associated with his work. Furthermore, *Tales and Fables* and *A Letter to the Most Insolent Man Alive* do not contain any author's name. This is strange, for by 1788 the name "Peter Pindar" was well known, and its insertion would have insured a greater sale; Wolcot was quite willing to have his minor pieces published, as *Pindariana* well illustrates. *The Cap* "printed by the author" is suspect for there was no need for Wolcot to publish his own material, and it is doubtful that he would use his own capital when others were willing to publish his work.

If these works were written by Wolcot, they would have been included in his collected works; but they are not. If anything, they are the works of some imitator, or imitators, attempting to gain some fortune by utilizing a pseudonym popular with the public.

SECONDARY SOURCES

GIDDY, EDWARD COLLINS. "A Biographical Sketch of the Late Doctor John Wolcot (Peter Pindar) Interspersed with Extracts from Some of His Letters." MS in Falmouth Public Library, Cornwall, England, c. 1827. Valuable account of Wolcot; contains only minor errors. Here are the only references to letters by Wolcot; includes material which has not been published.

GIRTIN, TOM. *Doctor With Two Aunts.* London: Hutchinson, 1959. Only full-length biography of the man; the author wisely mutes psychological approach. Although no footnotes are given for information, Mr. Girtin's facts can be trusted.

HOPKINS, KENNETH. *Portraits in Satire.* London: Barrie Books, 1958. Chapter on Peter Pindar offers a quick introduction to the satirist.

REITTERER, THEODOR. *Leben und Werke Peter Pindars (Dr. John Wolcot).* Wien and Leipzig: Wilhelm Braumüller, 1900. Superseded by the Girtin and Sinko studies; lists Wolcot's works translated into German.

SINKO, GRZEGORZ. *John Wolcot and His School: A Chapter from the History of English Satire.* Wroclaw: Place Wroclawskiego Towarzystwa Naukowego, 1962. A Marxist approach but valuable; Wolcot can be considered as a poet interested in the plight of the common man.

Index